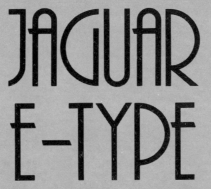

JAGUAR E-TYPE

3.8, 4.2 & 5.3-LITRE

Andrew Whyte

CONTENTS

ISBN 0 85429 370 1

A FOULIS Motoring Book

First published 1983

© **Haynes Publishing Group**

Published by:
Haynes Publishing Group
Sparkford, Yeovil,
Somerset BA22 7JJ

Distributed in USA by:
Haynes Publications Inc.
861 Lawrence Drive, Newbury
Park, California 91320, USA

Editor: Rod Grainger
Dust jacket design: Rowland Smith
Page Layout: Peter Kay
Dust jacket colour picture: In the
foreground the very last E-type
which was built early in 1975.
Behind is the very first type of 'E'
roadster as announced nearly 14
years earlier. The red roadster
is the predecessor of the 'E' –
the 1958-60 XK150S. Courtesy
Paul Skilleter
Endpaper picture: An early works
E-type Coupe used by the author
to cover the 1962 Tour de France.
Here the car is on the Pic du Midi
de Bigorre, above the Col du
Tourmalet
Colour photographs: Paul Skilleter
Road tests: Courtesy of *Motor* &
Autocar
Printed in England by: J.H.Haynes
& Co. Ltd

Titles in the *Super Profile* series

BSA Bantam (F333)
MV Agusta America (F334)
Norton Commando (F335)
Honda CB750 sohc (F351)
Sunbeam S7 & S8 (F363)
BMW R69 & R69S (F387)

Austin-Healey 'Frogeye' Sprite (F343)
Ferrari 250GTO (F308)
Ford GT40 (F332)
Jaguar E-Type (F370)
Jaguar D-Type & XKSS (F371)
Jaguar Mk 2 Saloons (F307)
Lancia Stratos (F340)
Lotus Elan (F330)
MGB (F305)
*MG Midget & Austin-Healey Sprite
(except 'Frogeye') (F344)*
Morris Minor & 1000 (ohv) (F331)
Porsche 911 Carrera (F311)

B29 Superfortress (F339)
Boeing 707 (F356)
Harrier (F357)

Further titles in this series will be published at
regular intervals. For information on new titles
please contact your bookseller or write to the
publisher.

FOREWORD

The E-type Jaguar was an all-time great motor car. Based on a racing car design it was, in many ways, the ideal road car. I cannot think of a parallel today; such a sequence of events probably couldn't happen ever again.

Its concept was, as with all Jaguars of the period, the work of Sir William Lyons; but it did not emerge from a totally original idea. Very few cars are totally original.

In creating a new competition car shape for Jaguar in 1953, former aircraft airflow engineer Malcolm Sayer had looked at several cars and in particular the Alfa Romeo *disco volante*. Lyons did not accept the first version, and Jaguar continued to race its C-type; then came the beautiful D-type of 1954, and it dominated Le Mans for three years.

At the time it seemed difficult to develop the 'D' into a road car, and indeed Sir William had a number of different mock-ups to consider. His old sports car range, revered as it was, continued into obsolescence while the definitive new design was being settled.

The XK150 may have seemed really old-fashioned when the E-type was finally launched at the Geneva show in March 1961; its successor made up for that in no uncertain terms, being a giant leap forward.

The E-type had a run of nearly ten years in six-cylinder form; then it had a kind of stay-of-execution as a V12, to give it a lifespan of some fourteen years. By that time it was not so much fashion as the law that suddenly made the 'E' seem obsolete.

In its original form, and fitted with appropriate tyres and axle ratio, the 3.8-litre car was good for over 150mph which naturally, became the goal for its successors. By the early seventies, the extra frontal area, and the weight, could not be overcome by the power of the silky smooth new V12 Jaguar engine for all its 5.3-litres. Emission laws in Jaguar's major export market, the USA, were partly responsible for the V12's design and the cars were also influenced by new safety regulations. The last E-types suffered particularly in this respect.

The XJ-S of today (announced in 1975) is not a sports car in the traditional sense. Thus the E-type is the last of the true sports Jaguars. Or is it?

Its following is enormous and shows no sign of waning. Many people have helped me in compiling this *Super Profile*. At the factory, Alan Hodge, Roger Clinkscales, and their staff have been of great assistance with photographs and the photography of cars in the works collection. Fellow scribe Paul Skilleter kindly reverted to his photographic role to produce many essential pictures specially to illustrate certain 'E' aspects.

As always, the Jaguar Drivers' Club has come to the aid of this particular party. E-type Register stalwarts George Gibbs, Alan Hames, and Gordon Skelton have all spent considerable time talking to me about E-type ownership today. Their own cars are an example to all.

Above all, every E-type enthusiast owes a debt of gratitude to Jaguar founder Sir William Lyons, technical director Bill Heynes, and power unit chief Walter Hassan and their colleagues for providing the world with an unforgettable motoring machine.

E-type production petered out in the mid-seventies when Jaguar was losing its identity as a company, plunged into the gloom of BL's misguided efforts to emulate Ford or GM, or both. The marque sometimes seemed destined for extinction and it was not until 1980 that truly positive steps were taken to catch Jaguar as it fell from the pedestal it had occupied for so long. One area of Jaguar which had never lost its continuity of purpose in the dark days was Engineering. Only a team capable of designing and building a car such as the E-type could have hoped to keep its head above water. Now, in the eighties, Jaguar is a company with its own head man once again; the team has responded to John Egan's positive leadership, and once again Jaguar cars can take their place among the finest in the world. The once close-knit teams that created Rovers, MGs and Triumphs are long-gone. The names may live on, and the cars may be good, but the soul has been destroyed. The E-type epitomises the special nature of Jaguar, the one marque to emerge in all its glory now that most of the 'Lessons of Leyland' have been well and truly learned. Perhaps there *will* be a true successor one day, after all?

Andrew Whyte

HISTORY

Henry Manney III, one of the world's most entertaining and astute motoring writers described it as "The Greatest Crumpet-Catcher Known to Man".

An American Europhile, he wrote thus for his UK audience: "... I have driven many cars here, there and everywhere, getting more than my share of appraising looks, and as I am an ugly and hairy old man I have never taken them for my benefit. Conducting the E-type roadster I got enough dark looks to curl my hair; two birds actually tried to pick me up, and fur-faced Jenkinson (owner of a red coupe) even claims that girls smile at *him*. The Jaguar advertising boys have been barking up the wrong tree with their grice, spice, and pice. All they need to point out is ... 'If You Want To Get Laid, Buy a Jaguar'. Then all Sir William would need to do is take over BMC's factories and turn out Es like bread rolls".

Manney wrote that in 1965. He must have felt he'd been psychic when, within a year, Jaguar's founder and Chairman Sir William Lyons got up with Sir George Harriman (boss of the then British Motor Corporation) to say in duet: "We are pleased to announce the successful completion of negotiations ... the merger is both logical and beneficial to both parties". Just before that, I had navigated Henry Manney on his first, brief test of the new 2+2. This time he was writing for his US readers. His *Road & Track* report concluded: "... as for crumpet catching – as the front seats now recline into that extra room, a girl ain't safe noplace, is she?"

Within two years, of course, the resultant company BMH – British Motor Holdings – became the poor relation when Sir Donald Stokes effected the next stage in the building of the colossus that is BL. (Or rather, *was* – for the signs have been, for some time, that a return to companies of comprehensible size is taking place). Fortunately for Henry Manney's prediction and for long-term history, Jaguar lived through the seventies and survived to fight again, as it is doing so successfully, now that it has its own captain and crew.

***

It is not difficult to be frivolous about the image of the E-type Jaguar, a product of the 'Swinging Sixties'. So many eulogies have been prepared in its honour. Denis Jenkinson, renowned Continental Correspondent of *Motor Sport* and the butt of Manney's foregoing penmanship, used to run Porsches. Afterwards he ran his E-type coupe; then he replaced it with a roadster. His recent book on the subject ends simply: "Not all Jaguar cars have had classic status, but nobody will dispute the E-type being a classic. When it appeared in 1961 it set new standards in motoring, and its performance is still a yardstick today. In its 14-year production run it maintained its looks from start to finish, which says everything for the design team that created the greatest Jaguar of all time".

Sir William would have understood that... but, "Crumpet-Catcher"? Ye gods!

***

Like most new Jaguars, the E-type was 'long-awaited' but still the scene-stealer when it appeared. Its launch was at that most international of motor shows, Geneva, in March 1961.

It *could* be said that it had been seen *originally* nearly seven years earlier, when Jaguar – at the height of its fame in sports-car racing – brought its D-type to Le Mans for the 24-hour race. Here it should be stated that the D-type's predecessor, the C-type, had been a competition version of the famous XK120 sports car which took the first post-war Earls Court motor show (1948) by storm ...hence the 'C' designation. No one had thought of an official name for its successor, so it became known around the experimental department of the new Browns Lane works in Coventry as the 'D'. The name stuck, so when the rumours started to circulate about a successor to the XK series of sports car for the road, it was almost a foregone conclusion. Sure enough, "E-type" it was.

***

The story of the D-type is told in another *Super Profile*. Suffice it to say that the car won a hat-trick of victories at Le Mans, in the gruelling 24-hour race, to become the most successful of *all* British cars in that famous event. (Even today, only those two most consistent of all sports-racing car makers, Ferrari and Porsche, have bettered Jaguar's Le Mans record of wins and places.)

The regulations placed a 3-litre limit from 1958, and the Jaguars (no longer works-entered anyway) failed, largely due to lack of a developed engine of that size. Then in 1960, three years after Jaguar's fifth and last win, the American millionaire sportsman, Briggs Cunningham, persuaded Jaguar to let him enter a prototype Jaguar with an alloy-block 3-litre version of the XK engine. Fast in practice and in the race (if sporadically), the smooth Jaguar, nowadays called 'E2A' but nameless then, retired as problem upon problem piled up. The car raced in America several times (as a '3.8') later that year, taking a first and a third; then it was shipped back to Coventry, rarely used and normally hidden under a dustsheet. Rumours that it was to be broken up persuaded Jaguar's Managing Director Lofty England to agree to its sale in the late sixties. E2A had made only rare public appearances. Now it is in the private Griffiths collection.

As 1960 wore on, the rumours got more and more frequent. Jaguar were being seen as a successful company. They had tidied up their brilliant compact range (by now called Mark 2 – see *Super Profile* by Paul Skilleter) and in the summer the company's acquisition of the Daimler factory had been announced. What about those long-in-the-tooth GT cars, the XK150s, though?

The answer came to Geneva in March 1961; there Sir William Lyons launched his new E-type roadster and coupe. Nothing quite like them had ever been offered for sale to the general public, and the price (little more than £2000 including UK tax) made them more attainable that any of their rivals.

At first the new car was available abroad only; but it was not long before the E-type was catching crumpet worldwide. *Oh, Henry Manney!*

***

The D-type had been a revolution, back in 1954; but new ideas are expected of competition cars.

Its most exciting technical feature had been its structure. The original XK120 had had an old-fashioned heavy chassis; the XK120C, or C-type, had been given a spaceframe for lightness. Its successor was quite different again, and it established the monocoque or stressed-skin structure as part of motor-racing technology. In the D-type's case, it was the cockpit area that took the form of a fuselage. The engine – the trusty Jaguar XK, foundation of the whole Jaguar

racing project – was mounted into an arrow-shaped subframe attached to the bulkhead and along the monocoque's floor. The design, simplified for the E-type, became a classic of engineering adaption – for manufacture and for servicing.

E-type production was to vary considerably over the years. (It was to reach a peak rate of around 240 cars a week for a while in the late 1960s, but its weekly average – still outstanding for a car of this kind, during nearly 14 years – was just over 100). The production areas, which were relocated several times in different parts of the Coventry factory to fit in with the main work of saloon car manufacture, were cleverly arranged so as not to occupy too much space. This was aided by having a complete sub-assembly section where the engine, gearbox and front suspension were all fitted to their subframe, then hoisted up to the raised track where electrics, insulations, and all the other detail items, were being fitted to the uncluttered monocoque. There the subframe was bolted on, the propshaft coupled and, hey presto, you had a motor car.

Here it should be added that this proved less convenient when the V12 engine came along and, after some deliberation, it was decided that it was best made as a car *before* receipt of the engine which could be lowered-in reasonably conveniently if hung at the right angle.

The XK engine was, initially, a triple-carburetter 3.8-litre straight-port unit, already well proved in the later XK150S models. Its 265bhp was strictly a gross 'bench ideal' figure, but there was more than enough power coupled with the docility which Jaguar customers expected. Even the gearbox was largely forgiven; gearbox trouble was almost unheard-of in a Jaguar, so the long travel, the unsynchronised '1st', and slow change did not cause too many raised eyebrows among early customers. It was a small price to

pay for one of the most beautiful and fast cars the world had seen – and the handling and the stopping were a match, too.

The E-type was the first production Jaguar to have fully independent suspension, and it was not before time. The XKs had been splendid cars, but the high performance of the XK150S (three-carburetter) highlit the safe but ponderous behaviour of a non-independent leaf-sprung rear end. The E-type's arrival made some aspects of the XK150 seem antiquated overnight.

During the war, IRS had been tried by Jaguar on a small experimental military vehicle. It had been used again on a D-type (but only once raced in that form) and on E2A, the 1960 'Cunningham' competition car.

An even earlier prototype was a little aluminium car with the body structure numbered E1A. It had been built back in 1957, the year of the XK150's announcement. If its picture ever appeared in print between then and 1961 I never saw it; yet it covered great mileages, mainly in Wales, as part of the development programme. Even the editor of *Motor,* the late Christopher Jennings, was lent the car by Sir William who was pleased and reassured by the favourable reaction. It wasn't just the speed; it was the ride and the handling. Jaguar front suspension had been regarded as excellent since 1948, when the Mark Five saloon had appeared with double wishbones and torsion bar; basically, this remained unchanged – but in detail it was refined for the E-type, which had IRS too.

It is remarkable how few cars had IRS twenty-odd years ago. The E-type was not pioneering a principle, though; but it was a pioneer in its way. Jaguar's technical team, headed by William Heynes, solved the old traction and tramp problems in a novel way. They had learned from their experiments that to attach a suspension system straight on to

For production, then, a steel pressing was evolved to carry the rear suspension and be mounted to the body floor through rubber blocks. Here it should be mentioned that the development of various rubber compounds (*and* all other aspects of insulation of the interior of a car from the road) has been a major part of the work culminating in today's ultra-refined road cars. That work was very much the responsibility of Robert Knight and, latterly, Jim Randle – Bill Heynes's successive heirs to overlordship of Jaguar vehicle engineering. There can be no doubt that the E-type was the beginning of Jaguar's successful battle to make the XJ series the most refined cars on the road.

The rear suspension of the E-type may have been heavier than a manufacturer of out-and-out sports cars would have chosen; but the E-type, though it looked racy, was pure road car. The differential unit, containing slip-limiting clutches, was bolted to the pressed-steel mounting piece; this had a wide base, to which was attached a pair of beefy tubular arms running parallel to, and below, the halfshafts – ensuring parallelogram movement, and keeping the wheels in the same vertical plane at all times. The hub carriers were fabricated in aluminium. Radius arms ran forward to the body. The halfshafts ran between paired coil-spring enclosed damper units. All the rubber mountings were arranged so as to balance torque reaction, and indeed the whole geometry at the rear was somewhat reminiscent of formula racing cars – then completing the changeover from front to rear engine, incidentally – especially in the use of the driving member (the halfshaft) as the upper suspension link.

In the braking department, of course, Jaguar were already well known for their pioneering work on aircraft-type disc brakes. They may not have been *the* first into production, but that may be to their credit. The C-type from 1952 and then the D-type (which had them as standard) proved their inevitability for racing; the XK150 of 1957 and the other Jaguar models soon afterwards showed the value of Jaguar's principle; that discs should be applied to four wheels or not at all. (The popular car market did not come into Jaguar's sphere of thinking).

Early disc brakes, in the development of which Dunlop were so helpful to Jaguar, had three pairs of pads on each front wheel and two pairs of pads on each rear wheel – the thinking being based on 60/40 (front/rear) loading. By the time the E-type was launched nearly ten years later, the disc system was simpler and more efficient. Single, quick-change pads made sure that the calipers were of a reasonable size, and only the handbrake gave the impression of being an afterthought which of course it was; that changed too. Probably the only disappointment about the brake design was the use of an American vacuum booster. Not everyone was particularly keen on the Plessey pump which had served as a transmission-supplied aid to braking on the D-type; the same might be said of the Kelsey-Hayes unit which Dunlop made for the 'E' under licence. At the rear, the discs were mounted inboard, so heat was another problem; likewise the lack of protection from road grit. Much was learned in the early days, and many modifications were put in hand – starting with self-

adjustment of the handbrake. It was to be some time before the ability of the system to seize-up was reduced to reasonable proportions by the deflection of spray away from the moving parts. In due course, the E-type braking system achieved a high standard; but this is definitely an area in which the owner needs to seek expert advice – or to study the subject personally. The main dates of change are listed elsewhere in this book.

The Competition Story

Though not intended as a 'racer' the E-type was, inevitably, sent to the circuits by early owners.

Not only did the car's name and appearance suggest a continuation of the competition series, but the first few to be delivered to the home market went to customers already renowned for their race-track prowess with Jaguar saloon cars. Moreover, the term 'GT' was becoming part of the sports motorist's language, and *gran turismo* racing was reaching international level.

It was at the national spring meeting at Oulton Park, Cheshire, in April 1961, that the new Jaguar made its racing debut. There were two cars – one entered by Surrey distributor John Coombs for Roy Salvadori who led initially (but faltered as the brakes got hot and inconsistent) and the other by Tom Sopwith's *Equipe Endeavour* for wily Graham Hill, who won. A Ferrari 250GT split the Jaguars. Salvadori won shortly afterwards at Crystal Palace, and history therefore shows that the E-type was the winner of its first two races. There is a school of thought that suggests the E-type should have left racing alone thereafter. At international level, undoubtedly, the Ferrari 250GT reigned supreme, and its position at the top was strengthened by the introduction of that beautiful 'homologation

special', the 250GTO, for the 1962 season – the first season of the new GT race championship.

It is a moot point as to whether Jaguar's retaliation was a wise move or not. To continue to develop for racing is always good practice and good for morale at a motor factory. Times were changing rapidly, however, and the the structure was to bring about noise and harshness which were the very two characteristics it was Sir William Lyons's aim to eliminate – or at least reduce to a minimum. Jaguar action was too little, too late.

Throughout 1962, the Coombs E-type was developed and raced (usually by Graham Hill), and for 1963 a fairly definitive specification for competitions was established. Only a further dozen of these so-called 'lightweight' Es were built, no two being exactly alike. Maybe a few more were planned, for the immediately-subsequent numbers (850670 to 850675 inclusive) have been left blank in Jaguar's chassis record books.

The first 'lightweight' (chassis 850658) was sent across to the works competition department (as it was still being called) to take over the identity of the Coombs car (850006), which was the car on which the factory did its experiments. The next two (850659/60) were sent to the USA in time for the '63 Sebring 12-hour race in which they did finish, but well behind six Ferraris. Hill's skill, plus 1963's early-season shortage of much strong opposition, gave the Coombs/Works 'lightweight' victories at Snetterton, Goodwood, and Silverstone; a short but consistent sequence which made it seem as if the modified E-type *would* be a match for the GTO Ferrari; but it was not to be. Yet again, Ferrari dominated in the long term.

This is not to say that the E-type and its lighter variant were not fine cars. 850661 was purchased by C.T. Atkins for Roy Salvadori,

whose ability at the wheel of sports cars was without question; only a spin prevented him from winning at Silverstone, where he took the GT lap record. 850662 went to the German Jaguar importer, Peter Lindner, and his partner Peter Noecker won several races with it including one on Berlin's very fast Avus track; a first-lap lead in the Nurburgring 1000km race was not sustained, but it is still talked about!

Peter Lumsden and Peter Sargent shared the driving of 850663 to good effect, and Peter Sutcliffe took a good win at Montlhery with his car 850666. Two more (850664/5) went to Briggs Cunningham in the USA, but the American assault on Le Mans was not a success. Bob Jane won in Australia from time to time before putting 850667 out to grass. The other two 'regular' lightweight cars were sold originally to Dick Wilkins and Philip Scragg in the UK. There were several other E-types incorporating lightweight components, but the only one to be considered here is EC 1001, the special coupe which Dick Protheroe (a Jaguar dealer) prised out of Jaguar's engineering department. It had a steel centre-section (most lightweight Es had alloy engines *and* bodies) and a very beautiful fastback coupe body designed by Malcolm Sayer who had already created the shape of the C, the D, and the E-types. This was later copied when 850662's body was altered; sadly, Peter Lindner was killed at Montlhery in 1964 in this car, a replica of which (using some original components) was built in the early 'eighties by the skilled craftsmen of Lynx Engineering, members of the Jaguar Specalists' Association.

Factory interest in developing the E-type for competitions declined after this. There was a mid-engined car project by the mid-sixties – the XJ13 – and for a while this took priority. Different problems came after 1966 when Jaguar merged with BMC (soon to

become the 'poor relation' of British Leyland) which took effect in the summer of 1968.

In the meantime, however, the E-type, both modified and unmodified, became a serious contender in club racing, especially in the UK and USA.

This culminated in the mid-seventies with a most effective onslaught upon the Chevrolet Corvette-dominated American sports car championship scene, instigated by Jaguar's importing company and carried out by two very experienced teams – Joe Huffaker Engineering in the west and Group 44 in the east. Lee Mueller in the Huffaker car and Group 44 team boss Bob Tullius drove to regional championship victories in 1974, and the following year Tullius became USA national champion in his class to provide excellent publicity in the E-type's last selling year. Those two V12-engined cars created an excellent impression, but should not be allowed to overshadow the subsequent performances of a splendid USA effort by an Ohio-based team called *Gran Turismo Jaguar.* They continued to work on the six-cylinder E-type, winning many races. In recent years their British driver, Fred Baker, has brought them more success than ever, culminating in the 1980 national class championship at Road Atlanta, Georgia.

***

It is not in its racing history that the E-type Jaguar has proved the supreme, classic high-performance GT or road-going sports-car.

True, its whole concept stemmed from that of one of the great Le Mans winners; but it came at a time when the drivers of most cars designed for competition work were finding themselves in front of the engine rather than looking over it. As a *road-car* for the swinging 'sixties, however, there was never a car quite like the E-type; that's for sure ....

EVOLUTION

Like any car with a lifespan approaching fourteen years, the Jaguar E-type underwent many changes beneath the surface. The purpose of this section of the book is to list the more significant ones.

Dates of introduction are approximate and, in some cases, occurred at different times for different markets – particularly after the start of American exhaust emission and safety legislation.

Numbers built and chassis number identification will be found in the 'Specification' section.

Spring 1961: E-type roadster and fixed-head coupe models, in 2-seater form, introduced at Geneva motor show in March.
Autumn 1961: Self-adjusting handbrake; longer springs at rear; larger propshaft universal joints and rear hub-bearings; automatic fanbelt tensioner; internal bonnet locks.
Winter 1961/2: Improved brake master-cylinders and disc pad material; seatbelt attachments; better bonnet hinges; footwells in cockpit.
Summer 1962: Sealed propshaft universal joints; improved pedal positions and operation; forged (previously tubular) halfshafts and lower steering column; more effective handbrake; pressings modified to give increased

rearwards seat adjustment.
Autumn 1962: Various axle-ratio changes for different markets; sealed halfshaft joints; water deflectors to rear hubs.
Summer 1963: Further improvements to rear end – notably, thicker discs and improvements to calipers and handbrake; more axle ratio changes; radial ply tyres optional.
Winter 1963/4: Shrouds for halfshaft universal joints; roadster bootlid emergency opening facility (in event of cable failure, catch could now be reached via hole in number plate panel).
Autumn 1964: Increase in engine displacement from 3781cc to 4235cc; all-synchromesh gearbox; diaphragm clutch; better seats and more cockpit padding.
Spring 1965: Front disc shields; more axle ratio changes (3.07:1 now standardised for UK).
Winter 1965/6: Hazard warning standardised.
Spring 1966: Two-plus-two coupe added to range, with automatic transmission optional.
Autumn 1966: Modified clutch and brake operation.
Summer 1967: Streamlined headlamp covers deleted and headlamps moved forward slightly to meet first phase of new North American regulations; new type of spoked road wheels.
Winter 1967/8: "USA Federal" specifications introduced, with many revisions to body, gradually applying to all markets. (Cars in this period sometimes called "Series $1\frac{1}{2}$" in retrospect).
Autumn 1968: Series Two range introduced, with headlamps moved further forward; larger rear lamps; revised interior; more rake for 2+2's windscreen; larger air intake; steel wheels optional; power assisted steering optional, etc.

Winter 1968/9: Steering column lock standardised.
Autumn 1969: Redesigned cam profiles for quietness and longer service intervals.
Winter 1969/70: Camshaft covers drilled to take warm air duct, required by low-emission engines; ignition key alarm system (USA and Canada); ballast resistor ignition.
Spring 1971: Series Three range (roadster and 2+2 coupe only) introduced, with 5343cc twelve-cylinder engine (4235cc engine engineered into new model, and catalogued, but never offered for sale); long wheelbase, as original 2+2, now standard.
Summer 1972: Various improvements (mostly at this stage) included more suitable axle ratios, new (Waso) steering lock, fresh-air vents to footwells, etc.
Autumn 1973: Two-plus-two coupe discontinued.
Winter 1973/4: More modifications, with front and rear impact-absorbing bumpers spoiling looks of export models more than ever.
Autumn 1974: Last E-type roadsters constructed.
Winter 1974/5: Last E-type completed, followed by announcement of "The end of the line".

SPECIFICATION

Jaguar E-type 3.8-litre

Models	Open two-seater and fixed-head coupe two-seater.
Period Current	1961 to 1964
Numbers made	15,490 *(see full details at end of section)*.
Drive configuration	Front engine, rear wheel drive.
Engine	Jaguar 'XK' 6-cylinder, twin overhead camshaft, 3781cc, 87mm x 106mm engine with cast iron block and aluminium alloy cylinder head containing hemispherical combustion chambers. Triple SU HD8 carburetters. 265bhp gross at 5500rpm; 260lb/ft torque at 4000 rpm.
Transmission (manual)	Four-speed gearbox with synchromesh on top three ratios. Close ratio gearbox offered.
Transmission (automatic)	Not available.
Final drive	Hypoid, standard ratios were 3.31:1 or 3.07:1; others were 2.93, 3.54, 3.77, and 4.09:1
Suspension (front)	Independent by torsion bars, wishbones, telescopic dampers, and anti-roll bar.
Suspension (rear)	Independent by coil springs, radius arms, telescopic dampers, and anti-roll bar (lateral location through tubular links and fixed length halfshafts).
Steering	Rack and pinion; 2.75 turns lock-to-lock.
Brakes	Dunlop bridge-type disc front and rear.

Wheels and Tyres	Dunlop wire spoke wheels fitted with 6.40-15 inch Dunlop RS5 tyres (tubed). Dunlop R5 racing tyres listed as options.
Chassis & Body	Semi-integral steel structure, featuring detachable front subframe and monocoque cockpit area. Major pressings by Abbey Panels of Coventry; minor pressings and build-up by Jaguar Cars of Coventry.
Weight (approx)	24cwt (roadster) and 25cwt (f.h.coupe) unladen, with fluids and part-filled fuel tanks.
Dimensions	8ft.0in. wheelbase; 4ft.2in. track; 14ft.7.5in. length; 5ft.5.3in. width; 3ft.11in. height (soft top up) or 4ft.0in. (fixed head coupe).
Performance (approx) *(see road-tests for further details)*	0 to 50mph in 5.5 sec; 0 to 100mph in 17 sec; max: 150mph + (on R5 tyres); standing-start quarter-mile in 15 sec.
Price (UK)	March '61, roadster = £1480 (£2098 inc. tax), extra for hardtop £54 (£77 inc. tax); fixed head coupe = £1550 (£2197 inc. tax). * November 1962, roadster = £1513 (£1829 inc. tax); fixed-head coupe = £1583 (£1913 inc. tax).

* *Purchase tax was reduced 6/11/62.*

Jaguar E-type 4.2-litre

Models	Open two-seater, fixed head coupe and 2+2 coupe.
Period current	1964 to 1970 (2+2 from 1966; "Series Two" across range from 1968).
Numbers made	41,740 *(see full details at end of section).*
Engine	"XK", 4235cc, 93mmx106mm, 265bhp gross at 5400rpm; 283lb/ft torque at 4000 rpm. *(North American spec. later changed; see text).*
Transmission (manual)	Four-speed all-synchromesh gearbox.
Transmission (automatic)	Borg Warner Model 8 three speed optional on 2+2
Steering	Power assistance optional from "Series Two".
Brakes	Change from Dunlop to Girling manufacture in this period.
Wheels & Tyres	Pressed steel wheels optional on "Series Two". Radial-ply tyres introduced during this period.
Weight (approx)	27.5cwt. for 2+2; other models up fractionally.

Dimensions	2+2 = 9 inches longer and 2.5 inches higher than existing fixed head coupe.
Performance (approx)	2+2 (manual transmission): 0 to 50mph in 6 sec; 0 to 100mph in 19 sec; max: 140mph; standing-start quarter-mile in 15.5 sec.
Price (UK)	September 1964, roadster = £1558 (£1896 inc. tax); fixed head coupe = £1648 (£1993 inc. tax). March 1966, 2+2 coupe = £1857 (£2245 inc. tax). October 1968 Series Two (No increase for new models); roadster = £1655 (2117 inc. tax); fixed-head = £1740 (£2225 inc. tax); 2+2 coupe = £1922 (2458 inc. tax); 2+2 (auto) = £2042 (2611 inc. tax).

Jaguar E-type 5.3-litre

Models	Open two-seater (long wheelbase) and 2+2 coupe, designated "Series Three".
Period current	1971 to 1975 (2+2 discontinued 1973).
Numbers made	15,290 *(see full details at end of section).*
Engine	Jaguar V12, overhead camshaft (one per bank), 5343cc, 90mm x 70mm, all-alloy engine, with flat-base cylinder head and combustion chambers effectively built into piston crowns. Four Zenith-Stromberg 175 CDSE carburetters. 272bhp (DIN) at 5850rpm; 304lb/ft (DIN) torque at 3600rpm.
Transmission (manual)	As 4.2.
Transmission (automatic)	Borg Warner model 12 optional on all models.
Suspension (front)	Anti-dive geometry.
Suspension (rear)	Little change.
Steering	Rack and Pinion, power-assisted.
Brakes	Still Girling discs all round: front discs now of ventilated type.
Wheels & Tyres	Pressed steel 6-inch rim wheels standard; wire wheels optional. E70 VR-15 inch Dunlop radial ply tyres.
Weight (approx)	28.5cwt (roadster) and 29.5cwt (2+2).
Dimensions	8ft.9in. wheelbase; 4ft.6.5in. front track; 4ft.5in. rear track; 15ft.4.5in. length; 5ft.6.3in. width; 4ft.1in. height (soft top up) or 4ft.3in. (2+2 coupe).
Performance (approx) *(see road-tests for further details)*	9 to 50mph in 5 sec; 0 to 100mph in 16 sec; max: 145mph; standing-start quarter-mile in 14.5 sec.

Price (UK)

March 1971, roadster = £2510 (£3139 inc. tax); 2+2
coupe = £2708 (£3403 inc. tax).
*(Last roadster listing, in early 1975, was £3743 inc.
tax. That autumn, the XJ-S was introduced at more
than double the price. Inflation was on its way).*

Quantities and distribution

Model	Litres	Series	Chassis sequence from (no.) (RHD)	(LHD)	(Years)	Number Made (approx.): (RHD)	(LHD)	(Home)	(Export)	(Total)
	3.8	first	850001	875001	1961-64	940	6880	760	7160	7820
	4.2	first	1E1001	1E10001	1964-68	1180	8370	1050	8500	9550
Roadster	4.2	second	1R1001	1R7001	1968-70	780	7850	690	7940	8630
	5.3	third	1S1001	1S20001	1971-75	1870	6120	1740	6250	7990
								Total roadsters:		**33990**
	3.8	first	860001	875001	1961-64	1800	5870	1560	6110	7670
Fixed-head	4.2	first	1E2001	1E30001	1964-68	1960	5810	1700	6070	7770
coupe	4.2	second	1R20001	1R25001	1968-70	1070	3790	910	3950	4860
								Total fixed-heads:		**20300**
	4.2	first	1E50001	1E75001	1966-68	1380	4220	1220	4380	5600
2+2 coupe	4.2	second	1R35001	1R40001	1968-70	1040	4190	870	4460	5330
	5.3	third	1S50001	1S70001	1971-73	2120	5180	1830	5470	7300
								Total 2+2 coupes:		**18230**
								GRAND TOTAL of all E-types:		**72520**

ROAD TESTS

The Motor

THE MOTOR March 22 1961

Continental Road Test No. 10/61

Make: Jaguar **Type:** E-type

Makers: Jaguar Cars, Ltd., Coventry, England.

Test Data

CONDITIONS: *Weather: Dry, warm, wind negligible. (Temperature 63°F. Barometer 30.5 in. Hg.). Surface: Dry tarmacadam. Fuel: Italian "Super" grade pump petrol (98-100 Octane Rating by Research Method).*

INSTRUMENTS

Speedometer at 30 m.p.h.	6% slow
Speedometer at 60 m.p.h.	1% fast
Speedometer at 90 m.p.h.	1% fast
Speedometer at 120 m.p.h.	accurate
Distance recorder	2½% slow

WEIGHT

Kerb weight, (unladen, but with oil, coolant and fuel for approx. 50 miles)	24 cwt.
Front/rear distribution of kerb weight	51/49
Weight laden as tested	28 cwt.

MAXIMUM SPEEDS

Flying Quarter Mile

Mean of opposite runs	149.1 m.p.h.
Best one-way time equals	150.1 m.p.h.

"Maximile" speed. (Timed quarter mile after one mile accelerating from rest.)

Mean of opposite runs	136.4 m.p.h.
Best one-way time equals	136.4 m.p.h.

Speed in gears (at 5,500 r.p.m.)

Max. speed in 3rd gear	107 m.p.h.
Max. speed in 2nd gear	74 m.p.h.
Max. speed in 1st gear	40 m.p.h.

FUEL CONSUMPTION

(Direct top gear)

25 m.p.g. at constant 30 m.p.h. on level.
27 m.p.g. at constant 40 m.p.h. on level.
27½ m.p.g. at constant 50 m.p.h. on level.
27½ m.p.g. at constant 60 m.p.h. on level.
26½ m.p.g. at constant 70 m.p.h. on level.
24 m.p.g. at constant 80 m.p.h. on level.
22½ m.p.g. at constant 90 m.p.h. on level.
21 m.p.g. at constant 100 m.p.h. on level.
17½ m.p.g. at constant 110 m.p.h. on level.
14½ m.p.g. at constant 120 m.p.h. on level.
13½ m.p.g. at constant 130 m.p.h. on level.

Overall Fuel Consumption for 2,859 miles, 144.9 gallons, equals 19.7 m.p.g. (14.35 litres/100 km.).

Touring Fuel Consumption (m.p.g. at steady speed midway between 30 m.p.h. and maximum, less 5% allowance for acceleration) 21.3.

Fuel tank capacity (maker's figure). 14 gallons

STEERING

Turning circle between kerbs:

Left	39 ft.
Right	36½ ft.
Turns of steering wheel from lock to lock	2½

BRAKES from 30 m.p.h.

1.00 g retardation (equivalent to 30 ft. stopping distance) with 115 lb. pedal pressure.
0.96 g retardation (equivalent to 31 ft. stopping distance) with 100 lb. pedal pressure.
0.79 g retardation (equivalent to 38 ft. stopping distance) with 75 lb. pedal pressure.
0.49 g retardation (equivalent to 61 ft. stopping distance) with 50 lb. pedal pressure.
0.22 g retardation (equivalent to 136 ft. stopping distance) with 25 lb. pedal pressure.

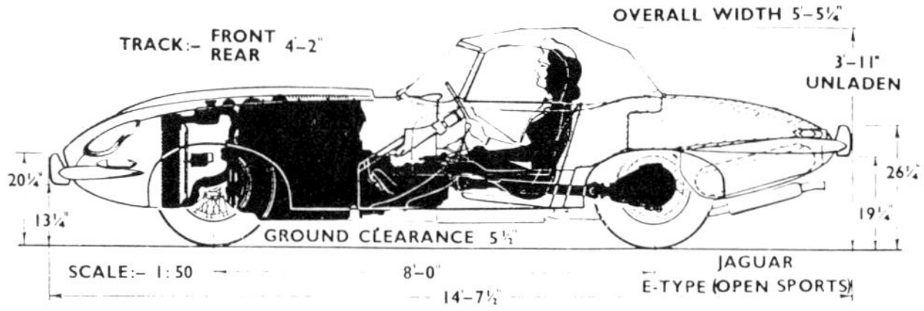
OVERALL WIDTH 5-5¼"
TRACK:- FRONT REAR 4-2"
3'-11" UNLADEN
20¼"
26½"
13¼"
19¼"
GROUND CLEARANCE 5½"
SCALE:- 1:50
8'-0"
14'-7½"
JAGUAR E-TYPE OPEN SPORTS

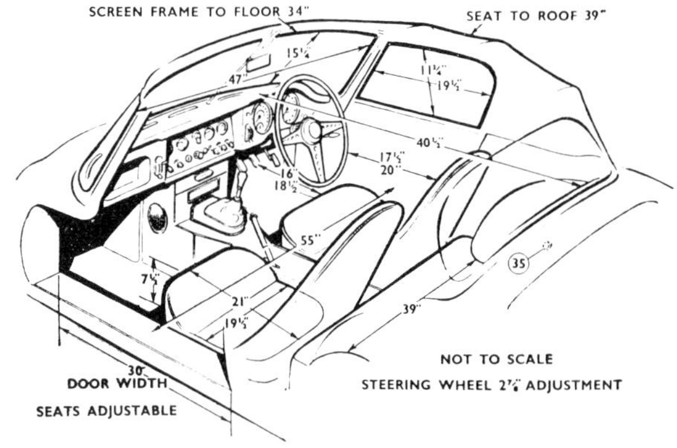
SCREEN FRAME TO FLOOR 34"
SEAT TO ROOF 39"
15¼
47
11¼"
19½"
40½"
17½"
20"
16"
18½
55"
35
7½"
21"
19½"
39"
NOT TO SCALE
30"
DOOR WIDTH
STEERING WHEEL 2⅞" ADJUSTMENT
SEATS ADJUSTABLE

ACCELERATION TIMES from standstill

0-30 m.p.h.	2.6 sec.
0-40 m.p.h.	3.8 sec.
0-50 m.p.h.	5.6 sec.
0-60 m.p.h.	7.1 sec.
0-70 m.p.h.	8.7 sec.
0-80 m.p.h.	11.1 sec.
0-90 m.p.h.	13.4 sec.
0-100 m.p.h.	15.9 sec.
0-110 m.p.h.	19.9 sec.
0-120 m.p.h.	24.2 sec.
0-130 m.p.h.	30.5 sec.
0-140 m.p.h.	39.3 sec.
Standing quarter mile	15.0 sec.

ACCELERATION TIMES on Upper Ratios

	Top gear	3rd gear
10-30 m.p.h.	5.6 sec.	4.2 sec.
20-40 m.p.h.	5.6 sec.	4.3 sec.
30-50 m.p.h.	5.4 sec.	4.0 sec.
40-60 m.p.h.	5.4 sec.	4.0 sec.
50-70 m.p.h.	5.3 sec.	3.9 sec.
60-80 m.p.h	5.0 sec.	3.7 sec.
70-90 m.p.h.	5.2 sec.	4.2 sec.
80-100 m.p.h.	5.7 sec.	4.8 sec.
90-110 m.p.h.	6.6 sec.	6.5 sec.
100-120 m.p.h.	7.7 sec.	—
110-130 m.p.h.	10.4 sec.	—
120-140 m.p.h.	15.1 sec.	—

HILL CLIMBING at sustained steady speeds

Max. gradient on top gear	1 in 5 (Tapley 440 lb./ton)
Max. gradient on 3rd gear	1 in 3.7 (Tapley 585 lb./ton)
Max. gradient on 2nd gear	1 in 2.4 (Tapley 860 lb./ton)

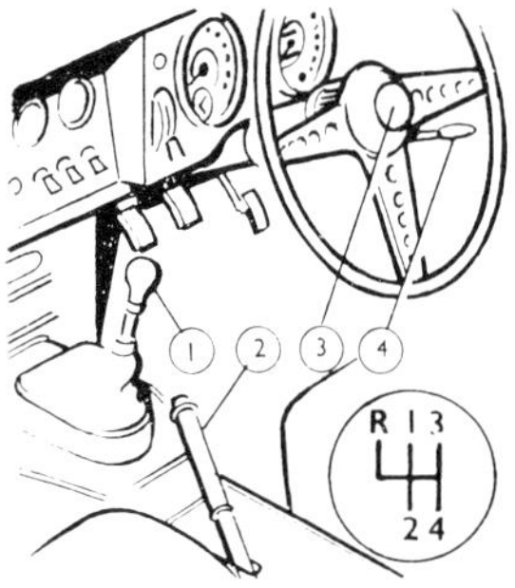
1
2
3
4
R 1 3
2 4

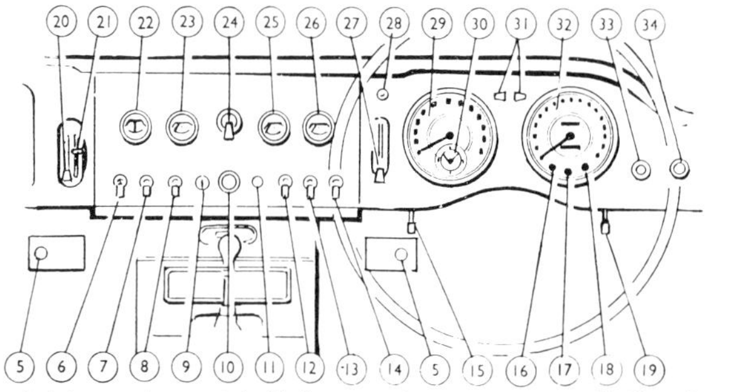
20 21 22 23 24 25 26 27 28 29 30 31 32 33 34
5 6 7 8 9 10 11 12 13 14 5 15 16 17 18 19

1, Gear lever. 2, Handbrake. 3, Horn button. 4, Direction indicator and headlamp flasher control. 5, Vent flaps. 6, Interior lights switch. 7, Bright-Dim panel light switch. 8, 2-speed heater fan control. 9. Ignition switch. 10, Cigar lighter. 11, Starter 12, Map light switch. 13, 2-speed windscreen wipers control. 14, Electric screen washer control. 15, Clock adjuster. 16, Ignition warning light. 17, Fuel warning light. 18, Headlamp warning light. 19, Trip reset. 20, Fresh air control. 21, Heater control. 22, Ammeter. 23, Fuel gauge. 24, Lights switch. 25, Oil pressure gauge. 26, Water thermometer. 27, Choke. 28, Choke warning light. 29, Rev counter. 30, Clock. 31. Direction indicator warning lights. 32, Speedometer. 33, Handbrake and hydraulic fluid level warning light. 34, Dip switch. 35, Boot lid control (see middle drawing).

THE MOTOR

—The JAGUAR E-type

Roadholding
and Handling
to Match a
Startling
Performance

The characteristic Jaguar grille has gone and the functional elegance of the frontal treatment gives little encouragement to badge and spotlight collectors.

WHEN one of the finest engine designs of the present time, in its most highly developed production form, is installed in a fully independently sprung chassis which has been evolved well beyond the final development of a series of Le Mans winning cars, the result should be something of a landmark in sports-car progress. Three thousand miles at home and abroad in little more than a week have convinced us that this expectation is more than justified.

Curiously enough, its very close connection in design and appearance with competition Jaguars gives people the impression that this is essentially a racing car with all the limitations for ordinary use that this implies. Nothing could be farther from the truth; admittedly it is quite easily the fastest car ever tested by *The Motor* but the roadholding is entirely capable of handling the power, the springing is more comfortable than that of many sober touring cars and the engine is extremely flexible and devoid of temperament. The ease and delicacy of control is such that 220 b.h.p./ton was no embarrassment at all on the packed snow and ice of Swiss mountain passes using ordinary racing tyres.

A good medium-powered family saloon will accelerate from 10-30 m.p.h. in top gear in about 10-11 sec. The E-type will do 110-130 m.p.h. in this time and, despite its very high top gear, 10-30 m.p.h. in half the time; on one occasion it climbed Birdlip hill (maximum gradient 1 in 6) in top, travelling quite slowly and using only part throttle. This initial rate of acceleration, about 4 m.p.h. every second, is maintained in one steady effortless sweep all the way up to 100 m.p.h., but for real exhilaration when emerging from a 30 m.p.h. speed limit, second gear will spin the speedometer needle round to the mid-

seventies in about 7 sec. to the accompaniment of a very subdued but delightfully hard exhaust hum and considerable strain on the neck muscles, whilst another 6 sec. in third brings up the hundred.

This exceptional combination of full-range torque and very high maximum output is complemented by smoothness and mechanical silence of a very high order. It should be said, however, that the engine in our test car used oil at the rate of about 1,300 m.p.g. when driven hard and that towards the end of a journey across London in the rush hour some fluffiness was noticeable due to sooting of the standard grade plugs. The 9 : 1 compression ratio caused a trace of pinking in the 2,000-2,500 r.p.m. band even with 100-octane fuel.

With the exception of bottom, the gears are quiet and the ratios extremely well selected, but the synchromesh is much less powerful than is now usual. With a clutch that has a fairly long travel and does not free perfectly, this means that really quick upward changes from first to second, and to a lesser extent, from second to third, cannot be made silently at high revs, whilst high-speed downward changes demand fairly accurate double declutching; the movement of the gearlever is rather heavy. "Heel and toe" operation of brake and throttle is possible but difficult.

In Brief

Price (as tested) £1,480, plus purchase tax £617 15s. 10d., equals £2,097 15s. 10d.
Capacity ... ... 3,781 c.c.
Unladen kerb weight ... 24 cwt.
Acceleration:
  20-40 m.p.h. in top gear ... 5.6 sec.
  0-50 m.p.h., through gears 5.6 sec.
Maximum direct top gear gradient 1 in 5
Maximum speed ... 149.1 m.p.h.
"Maximile" speed ... 136.4 m.p.h.
Touring fuel consumption ... 21.3 m.p.g.
Gearing: 24.8 m.p.h. in top gear at 1,000 r.p.m. (Based on tyre dia. at 100 m.p.h.) 35.6 m.p.h. at 1,000 ft./min. piston speed.

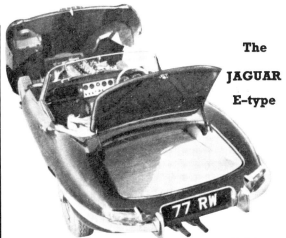

The JAGUAR E-type

Both bonnet and boot lid are spring counterbalanced in the open position and the former provides exceptional access to the engine and front suspension. The folded hood is normally enclosed by a neat cover. By undoing two thumb screws the central instrument and switch panel can be hinged down to expose the wiring and all the fuses.

On the standard 3.31 to 1 final drive ratio the car proved undergeared for maximum speed. On our timed runs with the hood up it flattened out around 150 m.p.h., about 6,000 r.p.m. This is well beyond the engine speed for peak power, nominally 5,500 r.p.m. but probably less as installed, so that the optional higher axle ratio would produce an even higher maximum.

The Dunlop Road Speed RS5 tyres, which are standard equipment on the Jaguar, have been used by test drivers for short bursts up to 150 m.p.h., but it was considered highly desirable that maximum speed runs should be made on the R5 racing covers that are offered as optional extras. At 100 m.p.h. these give a rolling radius for the driving wheels some 4½% greater than that of the standard tyres.

Clearly it would be absurd to present a set of performance figures which could be obtained by using one type of tyre for top speed and fuel consumption and another of different size for optimum acceleration. All the figures in the data panel were therefore recorded on R5 covers, although a later check on Road Speeds showed slightly better initial acceleration which reduced the standing quarter mile to 14.7 sec.

The Jaguar has exceptional brakes, although despite the use of a vacuum servo, the pedal loads are fairly high, so that there is an initial impression of a lack of "bite" which the tabulated figures show

to be misleading. During a considerable part of the test the brakes were spoiled by a most obscure fault which gradually allowed air to leak into the rear hydraulic circuit giving excessive pedal travel.

Before we had driven the E-type very far it became clear that the new independent rear suspension was a major step forward which had put the road manners of the car into the highest category. The springing is quite soft and provides a most comfortable ride; at high speeds on bumpy roads very few touring cars can compete with it in this respect and certainly not in the tremendous feeling of security and stability with which it deals with sudden

---

Specification

Engine

Cylinders	6
Bore	87 mm.
Stroke	106 mm.
Cubic capacity	3,781 c.c.
Piston area	55.3 sq. in.
Valves	Overhead (twin o.h.c.)
Compression ratio	9/1
Carburetters	Three 2 in. S.U. H.D.8
Fuel pump	Lucas electric type 2FP
Ignition timing control	Centrifugal and vacuum
Oil filter	Tecalemit full-flow
Max. power (gross)	265 b.h.p.
at	5,500 r.p.m.
Piston speed at max. b.h.p.	3,820 ft./min.

Transmission

Clutch	10 in. Borg & Beck s.d.p.
Top gear (s/m)	3.31
3rd gear (s/m)	4.25
2nd gear (s/m)	6.16
1st gear	11.18
Reverse	11.18
Propeller shaft	Hardy Spicer open
Final drive	Hypoid bevel with PowrLok differential
Top gear m.p.h. at 1,000 r.p.m.	24.8
Top gear m.p.h. at 1,000 ft./min. piston speed	35.6
(based on racing tyre dia. at 100 m.p.h.)	

Chassis

Brakes	Dunlop disc all round
Brake disc diameter:	
Front	11 in. dia.
Rear	10 in. dia.
Friction area	31.8 sq. in. of friction material operating on 461 sq. in. rubbed area of discs

Suspension:
Front ... Independent by transverse wishbones, torsion bars and anti-roll bar
Rear ... Independent by lower wishbone, stressed articulated half-shafts and trailing link with coil springs and torsion anti-roll bar

Shock Absorbers:
Front ... Girling telescopic
Rear ... Twin Girling telescopic each side
Steering gear ... Rack and pinion
Tyres:
Dunlop RS5 6.40 × 15
or (as optional extra)
Dunlop Racing R5 6.00 × 15 front 6.50 × 15 rear

Coachwork and Equipment

Starting handle	No
Battery mounting	Under bonnet on left side
Jack	Manual 3-stage screw jack
Jacking points	One centrally each side

Standard tool kit: Adjustable spanner, screwdriver, pliers, plug spanner, 3 box spanners, 4 o.e. spanners, grease gun, hub mallet, tyre gauge, distributor screwdriver, feeler gauge, valve extractor.
Exterior lights: 2 headlights, 2 sidelights/flashers, 2 tail/stop lamps/flashers, number plate lamp.

Number of electrical fuses	8
Direction indicators	Amber flashers
Windscreen wipers:	3 blade, two speed, self-parking electric
Windscreen washers:	Lucas electric
Sun visors	None

Instruments: Speedometer with total and trip distance recorders, combined rev. counter and clock, water temperature gauge, ammeter, oil pressure gauge, fuel contents gauge.
Warning lights: Direction indicators, fuel level, brake fluid level and handbrake, headlamp main beam, choke.

Locks:	
With ignition key	Doors
With other keys	None
Glove lockers: One (open) on passenger's side of facia	
Map pockets	None
Parcel shelves:	One beneath rear window
Ashtrays	One below centre of facia
Cigar lighters	One

Interior lights: Map light under facia and light on rear bulkhead
Interior heater: Standard fresh-air heater/demister with two-speed fan
Car radio: H.M.V. Radiomobile (optional extra)
Extras available: Radio, R5 racing tyres, hardtop (detachable)

Upholstery material	Vaumol leather hide
Floor covering:	Carpet with felt underlay
Exterior colours standardized: 14 plus special colours at extra cost	
Alternative body styles:	Fixed head coupé

Maintenance

Sump: 11 pints, S.A.E. 30 (Summer), 20 (Winter) (13 pints, including filter)

Gearbox	2¼ pints, S.A.E. 30
Rear axle	2¼ pints, S.A.E. 90 (Hypoid)
Steering gear lubricant	Grease
Cooling system capacity	22 pints (2 drain taps)

Chassis lubrication: By grease gun every 2,500 miles to 22 points

Ignition timing	10° b.t.d.c.
Contact-breaker gap	.014 to .016 in.
Sparking plug type	Champion N.5
Sparking plug gap	.025 in.

Valve timing: Inlet opens 15° b.t.d.c. and closes 57° a.b.d.c. Exhaust opens 57° b.b.d.c. and closes 15° a.t.d.c.

Tappet clearances (cold): Inlet .004 in. Exhaust .006 in.
Wheel toe-in. Front 1/16 to 1/8 in., rear 0 to 1/8 in.
Camber angle: Front, 0 to ½ deg. positive, rear ¼ to 1 deg. negative

Castor angle	1½ to 2 deg.
Steering swivel pin inclination	4 deg.

Tyre pressures:

	Normal use		
Front	RS5 23 lb.	Rear	30 lb.
Front	R5 30 lb.	Rear	30 lb.
	Very high speed		
Front	RS5 30 lb.	Rear	35 lb.
Front	R5 35 lb.	Rear	40 lb.

Brake fluid	S.A.E. 70 R3
Battery type and capacity: 12 volt, 57 amp. hr.	

colonial sections encountered at really high speed. Much softer damper settings can be used in the absence of an unruly live rear axle and this eliminates a lot of vertical motion.

Travelling fast across Northern France we discovered that the extra width of the R5 rear tyres was causing them to foul on the wheel arches and restrict the bump movement of the rear suspension. We understand that this will be corrected in future, but in any case it does not arise with the normal tyres; with these it was very difficult to bottom the rear suspension on its rubber stops in this country, except by travelling extremely fast over switchback sections.

Any idea that rack and pinion steering is suitable only for small, light cars is contradicted by the Jaguar. Despite high gearing (2½ turns of the wheel covers the not very good lock) there is practically no trace of kickback, and the characteristic virtues of precision, smoothness and lightness are present to an outstanding degree. Even manoeuvring needs only a moderate effort, and for directional stability at speed the car has few rivals.

A great deal of clever development must have been required to produce cornering characteristics which are not only outstandingly good but particularly well suited to the unusual power-to-weight ratio. It is basically very near to being a neutral steering car, but the driver is constantly astonished by the amount of power he can pile on in a corner without starting to bring the tail round; as with front-wheel drive, hard acceleration through a bend is the right technique, and lifting off suddenly gives a marked oversteering change. Naturally, the power technique can be overdone in the lower gears, but this merely increases the nose-in drift angle in a most controllable way. It is possible to go on increasing the sideways "g" value to a quite surprising level, because the E-type retains its balance far beyond the point at which most sports cars have lost one end. The very low build (we only realized how low when we

saw a small foreign GT coupé towering over it) and anti-roll bars at both ends keep the roll angles right down, and it seems natural to throw the car about in a manner usually reserved for smaller and lighter sports cars.

For this kind of driving we found that the highest recommended pressures (30 lb. front, 35 rear) gave the most pleasant feel with Road Speed tyres at the expense of only a little more harshness on bad roads. The structure is so rigid that there is no trace of the bonnet movement and scuttle shake which plague so many open cars, and the suspension is very effectively rubber insulated. As a result, even racing tyres at maximum speed pressures, which are notorious for their extreme harshness and noisiness, fail to destroy the pleasure of road motoring, and they enhance the cornering power even further.

Habitability

As a long-distance grand touring car, the open Jaguar needs further development before it reaches quite the same high standard. Luggage accommodation is limited by the shallowness of the boot, and the imperfect fit of the hood round the winding glass windows leads to wind noise but not to draughts. In fact, for a soft-top car the wind noise is low, but in relation to its tremendously high cruising speed it could well be lower still. Averaging some 400 miles a day for six days with over 500 miles packed into one or two, we found the seats unsatisfactory. The squabs are effectively concave where they should be convex to support the small of the back and the cushions are rather hard and flat so that one tends to slide forward. The positions of the pedals and of the very attractive wood-rimmed steering wheel on its telescopic column are such as to provide any driver up to about 5 ft. 10 in. with a good arm's-length driving position and excellent visibility over a bonnet which looks much shorter from inside than it really is. Seat adjustment is not adequate for most taller people and neither is the headroom with the rather upright sitting position.

Ventilation is also a critical factor for long-distance comfort. In cool or mild weather the fresh-air intake through the heater system is adequate but the inside of the car can become rather hot in warm sunny weather even when the very quiet two-speed fan is used. Opening either window between 40 and 60 m.p.h. causes a low-frequency pressure fluctuation which makes the hood drum very loudly, and if the tank is more than three-quarters full petrol fumes are drawn in.

One solution, of course, is to lower the hood, which is a very quick and easy operation involving only three toggle catches and giving reasonably draught-free motoring irrespective of whether the side windows are wound up or down. The central hood-fixing toggle is connected to a slender tension rod running down to the scuttle in order to relieve the screen top rail of aerodynamic loads and the rear-view mirror is mounted on this rod. When the hood is down the loss of tension allows the rod to flex and the mirror to shake about.

At night the Le Mans-type headlights were not really adequate for the performance. There was insufficient spread to illuminate the sides of twisty roads and the dipped beams seemed to cause considerable annoyance to other road users.

The car we tested was the first open model to be completed and it was assembled and tested in considerable haste as we stood by to snatch it away. It is not surprising therefore that many body details such as door and bonnet locks left something to be desired and much development is still going on. It is difficult to see, however, how this car can fail to be a tremendous success. The sheer elegance of line which Jaguar seem able to produce by total disregard for fashion trends is allied to a combination of performance, handling and refinement that has never been equalled at the price and, we would think, very seldom surpassed at any price.

MOTOR   week ending October 31 1964

" . . . a combination of performance, handling, looks and refinement . . . still unequalled at the price."

Number 42
MOTOR TESTED
3020 MILES

JAGUAR E-type 4·2
Extended Test

PRICE
£1,648 plus purchase tax of £344 17s. 11d.
equals £1,992 17s. 11d.

How they run . . .

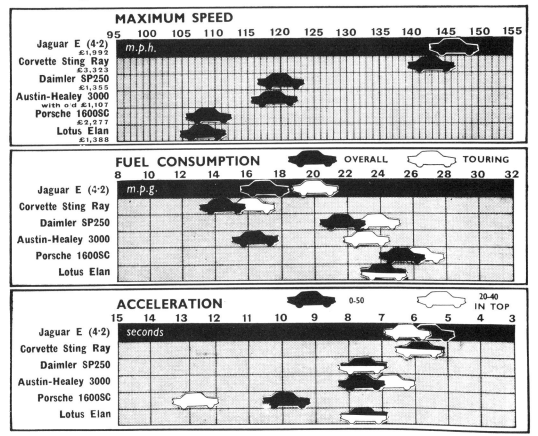

MAXIMUM SPEED

m.p.h. 95 100 105 110 115 120 125 130 135 140 145 150 155

- Jaguar E (4·2) £1,992
- Corvette Sting Ray £3,323
- Daimler SP250 £1,355
- Austin-Healey 3000 with o/d £1,107
- Porsche 1600SC £2,277
- Lotus Elan £1,388

FUEL CONSUMPTION   ■ OVERALL   □ TOURING

m.p.g. 8 10 12 14 16 18 20 22 24 26 28 30 32

- Jaguar E (4·2)
- Corvette Sting Ray
- Daimler SP250
- Austin-Healey 3000
- Porsche 1600SC
- Lotus Elan

ACCELERATION   ■ 0-50   □ 20-40 IN TOP

seconds 15 14 13 12 11 10 9 8 7 6 5 4 3

- Jaguar E (4·2)
- Corvette Sting Ray
- Daimler SP250
- Austin-Healey 3000
- Porsche 1600SC
- Lotus Elan

Performance figures of 95 cars tested in the past two years will be found in the road test summary on page 152

THERE have always been a handful of exotic cars built throughout the world which, by their very cost and scarcity, inspire a detached awe from ordinary mortals who cannot afford them. On every count but cost, the E-type would be an obvious choice for the current *corps d'elite* but at £2,000 it creates its own unique position among the world's desirable cars with a combination of performance, handling, looks and refinement that, even after 3½ years' production, is still unequalled at the price. Development of this remarkable vehicle has never stopped and numerous detail improvements have been made since its debut at the Geneva Show in March, 1961. Now, a bigger 4·2-litre engine, new all-synchromesh gearbox, better brakes and seats, and other details, mark the first major change; the latest car supplements, rather than replaces, the unaltered 3·8, and was fully described in *Motor* of October 14.

The new 4·2-litre supersedes the earlier 3·8 as the fastest car *Motor* has tested, with a mean maximum of exactly 150 m.p.h.; this marginal increase (less than 1 m.p.h.) stems from a higher axle ratio rather than more power, which remains at 265 b.h.p. (gross). The 10 per cent increase in capacity is reflected lower down the rev band by a corresponding increase in torque (from 240 to 283 lb. ft.) which, despite the higher gearing and greater weight, gives almost identical acceleration to our previous test car: with the lower (3·31 : 1) axle used before, there would be an appreciably greater strain on one's neck muscles which is severe enough now, 100 m.p.h. being reached from a standstill in well under 20 seconds. Using the lowest axle ratio, Americans will benefit from a better low-end performance while British and Continental buyers have improved steady-speed fuel consumption and even more relaxed cruising (100 m.p.h. corresponds to 4,060 r.p.m.) without any sacrifice in speed or acceleration.

The biggest improvement is the all-new, all-synchromesh gearbox. Gone is the tough, unrefined box that had accumulated a certain notoriety, in favour of one that will undoubtedly establish a correspondingly high reputation: although the lever movement is still quite long, it is fairly light and very quick, the synchromesh being unbeatable without being too obstructive. A good box by any standards and excellent for one that must transmit so much power.

Handling, steering and brakes are of such a high order that sensible drivers will never find the power/weight ratio of 220 b.h.p. per ton an embarrassment: indeed, this is one of those rare high-performance cars in which every ounce of power can be used on the road. The new seats are a big improvement but lack sufficient rake adjustment to make them perfect for all drivers. Nevertheless, 3,000 test miles (many of them on the Continent) confirm that this is still one of the world's outstanding cars, its comfortable ride, low noise level and good luggage accommodation being in the best GT tradition.

Performance

PRECONCEIVED ideas about speed and safety are apt to be shattered by E-type performance. True, very few owners will ever see 150 m.p.h. on the speedometer but, as on any other car, cruising speed and acceleration are closely related to the maximum and it is these that lop not just seconds or minutes, but half hours and more, off journey times. Our drivers invariably arrived early in the E-type and the absurd ease with which 100 m.p.h. can be exceeded on a quarter mile straight never failed to astonish them: nor did the tremendous punch in second gear which would fling the car past slower vehicles using gaps that would be prohibitively small for other traffic.

From a standing start, you can reach the 30 m.p.h. speed limit in under 3 seconds, or the 40 m.p.h. mark in under 4 seconds, so it needs a wary eye on the instruments to stay inside the law. In either case, these speeds can be doubled in little over twice the times to whisk the car clear of other traffic at a derestriction sign. From 30 m.p.h., it takes under 15 seconds to reach 100 m.p.h. and there is still another 15 m.p.h. to go before top must be engaged. Up to 90 m.p.h., any given speed can be increased by 20 m.p.h. in 4–5 seconds using third, and in 5–7 seconds using top. Low-speed torque and flexibility are so good that you can actually start in top gear, despite a 3·07 : 1 axle ratio giving 24·4 m.p.h. per 1,000 r.p.m. Driving around town, this fascinating tractability can be fully exploited by starting in first or second and then dropping into top which, even below 30 m.p.h., is sufficiently lively to out-accelerate a lot of cars. Before the plugs were changed half way through our test for a similar set of Champion N5s, prolonged low-speed town work caused misfiring when higher speeds were resumed, but a short burst of high revs in second gear would usually cure this fluffiness.

Motorway cruising speeds are governed by traffic conditions rather than any mechanical limitations: on lightly trafficked roads we completed several relaxed journeys at over 110 m.p.h. on the Italian Autostrada and Belgian Autoroutes. Not unexpectedly, hill climbing is remarkably good, top gear pulling the car up slopes (up to 1 in 5·2) that reduce many another to a second gear crawl. First copes easily with a start on a 1-in-3 hill.

19

MOTOR   week ending October 31 1964

New bucket seats have generous adjustment for reach, very small adjustment for rake. Most drivers found them a little upright but comfortable. Central armrest conceals a useful box for stowing odds and ends.

JAGUAR
E-type 4·2

All this performance is accompanied by astonishingly little fuss, the engine remaining smooth and mechanically quiet at all times. The electronic rev counter is an essential instrument, for the human ear could not detect that 5,500 r.p.m. was anywhere near the suggested limit of this magnificent engine. Even 6,100 r.p.m.—corresponding to 150 m.p.h.—does not sound unduly strained.

Unlike other Jaguars, the E-type has a hand choke: cold starts are instant after a night out in the open and the engine pulls without hesitation or coughing, though on full choke (which is only needed momentarily) idling speeds are high. The new pre-engaged starter is much smoother and quieter than the old Bendix gear.

Running costs

AT FIRST sight, 18·5 m.p.g. overall sounds heavy, but in relation to the performance this is an excellent consumption: many smaller-engined cars with nothing like the same performance can barely match it. Gentle driving will obviously improve the figure but not by any significant amount, as there is less than 4½ m.p.g. difference between the consumptions at a steady 30 m.p.h. and a steady 80 m.p.h. Good aerodynamics, high gearing and an efficient engine account for this unusually flat consumption curve. Only the very best British 100 octane petrol will prevent pinking at low r.p.m.; on the best Belgian, French and Italian brands, it would knock loudly if the throttle was not eased down progressively. At 5s. 1d. a gallon, fuel bills work out at £13 14s. 6d. per 1,000 miles at the overall consumption, and £11 8s. at the touring consumption of 21·5 m.p.g.

M.p.g. over several typical journeys worked out like this:—

45 miles of motorway, average 107 m.p.h. ..	17·1 m.p.g.
8 miles through London's northern suburbs, average 22 m.p.h.	19·2 m.p.g.
50 mile cross-country journey, hard driving over various roads; 58 m.p.h. average	16·7 m.p.g.
Comparatively gentle cruising over quiet roads; 46 m.p.h. average	26·0 m.p.g.

At one time notoriously high, oil consumption has been checked by new oil control piston rings to around 400 miles per pint.

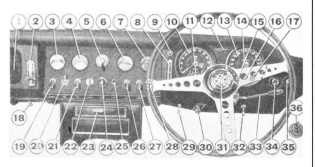

1, cubbyhole. 2, heater controls. 3, ammeter. 4, petrol gauge. 5, lights switch. 6, oil pressure gauge. 7, water thermometer. 8, choke. 9, choke warning light. 10, rev counter. 11, clock. 12, direction indicator warning light. 13, speedometer. 14, mileage recorder. 15, ignition light. 16, low fuel level warning light. 17, main beam warning light. 18, ventilator. 19, interior light. 20, panel light. 21, heater fan. 22, ignition key. 23, ashtray. 24, cigar lighter. 25, starter. 26, map light. 27, wipers. 28, screen washer. 29, clock adjuster. 30, ventilator. 31, horn. 32, trip re-set. 33, indicators and flasher. 34, handbrake on (and low fluid level) warning light. 35, dip switch. 36, bonnet.

Performance

Test Data: World copyright reserved: no unauthorized reproduction in whole or part.

Conditions: Weather: Dry and sunny, 12–18 m.p.h. breeze. (Temperature 54°–64°F, Barometer 30·07–30·02 in. Hg.) Surface: Dry tarmacadam. Fuel Super Premium grade pump petrol (101 octane by Research Method).

MAXIMUM SPEEDS

Flying kilometre

Mean of four opposite runs ..	150·0 m.p.h.
Best one-way time equals ..	150·0
"Maximile" Speed: (Timed quarter mile after 1 mile accelerating from rest)	
Mean of four opposite runs ..	136·2
Best one-way time equals ..	137·0
Speed in 3rd (at 5,500 r.p.m.)..	107
Speed in 2nd	78
Speed in 1st	51

ACCELERATION TIMES

From standstill

0-30 m.p.h.	..	..	..	..	2·7 sec.
0-40	..	..	..	..	3·7
0-50	..	..	..	..	4·8
0-60	..	..	..	..	7·0
0-70	..	..	..	..	8·6
0-80	..	..	..	..	11·0
0-90	..	..	..	..	13·9
0-100	..	..	..	..	17·2
0-110	..	..	..	..	21·0
0-120	..	..	..	..	25·2
0-130	..	..	..	..	30·5
Standing quarter mile			..		14·9

On upper ratios

				Top sec.	3rd sec.
10-30 m.p.h.	..	..	..	5·8	4·3
20-40	..	..	..	5·5	4·4
30-50	..	..	..	5·4	4·2
40-60	..	..	..	5·3	4·0
50-70	..	..	..	6·0	4·4
60-80	..	..	..	6·6	4·7
70-90	..	..	..	6·6	4·8
80-100	..	..	..	7·3	5·9
90-110	..	..	..	7·3	6·9
100-120	..	..	..	7·8	—
110-130	..	..	..	10·2	—

Overtaking
Starting at 40 m.p.h. in direct top gear, distance required to gain 100 ft. on another car travelling at a steady 40 m.p.h.=437 ft.

HILL CLIMBING

Max. gradient climbable at steady speed

					lb./ton
Top	..	..	1 in 5·2	..	(Tapley 420)
3rd	..	..	1 in 4·1	..	(Tapley 535)
2nd	..	..	1 in 2·8	..	(Tapley 745)

BRAKES

Deceleration and equivalent stopping distance from 30 m.p.h.

0·4 g with 25 lb. pedal pressure	.. 75 ft.
0·75 g with 50 lb. pedal pressure	.. 40 ft.
0·97 g with 60 lb. pedal pressure	.. 31 ft.
Handbrake	
0·44 g deceleration from 30 m.p.h.	.. 68¼

Brake Fade
TEST 1. 20 stops at ½ g deceleration at 1 min. intervals from a speed midway between 30 m.p.h. and maximum speed (=90 m.p.h.)

Pedal force at beginning	.. 25 lb.
Pedal force for 10th stop	.. 35

MOTOR   week ending October 31 1964

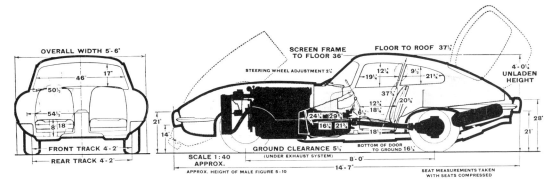

Released by two inside catches, the enormous bonnet tilts forward to reveal the whole of the engine and front suspension; an alternator and new induction manifolding are obvious changes. Accessibility for routine maintenance is excellent.

Transmission

WITH THE new gearbox in the 4·2, the slow deliberate change, weak synchromesh, and awkward engagement of first are things of the past. Instead, a lightweight lever can now be whisked into any gear as fast as the hand can move, without beating the new inertia-lock baulk-ring synchromesh. First gear still whines but not nearly so loudly and it can now be used to advantage for quick overtaking; the other ratios emit only a faintly audible hum. The new Laycock diaphragm clutch is much lighter than before and pedal travel reduced; although the movement is still quite long it is no longer essential to press the pedal to the floorboards when engaging first or changing gear. The clutch bites smoothly when moving off and will accept the brutality of racing changes without slipping and such is the low-speed torque that there is never any need to abuse the clutch for rapid take-offs, quick engagement at 2,000 r.p.m. giving the optimum results. High revs merely produce long black lines on the road, although we were always astonished at just how much power could be turned on without spinning the wheels.

Jaguar have reverted to the high 3·07 : 1 axle ratio as standard equipment for the home and European markets since it gives the fast, relaxed cruising speeds that are legally possible on our motorways, autobahns and autostradas. North American cars, restricted in top-end performance by low speed limits, have a much lower ratio that gives a lower maximum but considerably better acceleration.

Handling

ENORMOUS power in a relatively light chassis demands impeccable road manners. Developed from a famous line of Le Mans cars, it is not surprising to find the E-type's monocoque chassis and all-independent suspension are more than adequate for the power. The best technique is to accelerate round corners, weight transfer making the steering lighter and forcing the back down onto Dunlop RS5 tyres which have excellent adhesion on both wet and dry roads. They are, however, not really suitable for prolonged speeds above 140 m.p.h. and racing tyres were used for our maximum speed runs.

Cornering on an open throttle, even in a low gear, merely increases the drift angle as the car accelerates. Ultimately, the back will break away but in the dry it does so controllably and well beyond the point at which you think it should. In the wet, the accelerator must be treated with greater discretion. Even under severe cornering like this, the low build and anti-roll bars at each end keep roll angles to a minimum.

Positive medium-weight rack and pinion steering transmits plenty of feel through the wood-rimmed steering wheel, and some kick-back, too, on poor roads. High gearing—2¼ turns from poor lock to lock—and absence of understeer gives unusual responsiveness and swervability (especially on racing tyres which are otherwise rather harsh for normal motoring) and unlike some powerful cars, the E-type can be thrown about with confidence on twisty roads. At speed in a straight line, it is completely stable.

FUEL CONSUMPTION

Overall fuel consumption for 3,020 miles, equals 18·5 m.p.g. (15·4 litres/100 km.) Touring fuel consumption (m.p.g. at steady speed midway between 30 m.p.h. and maximum, less 5% allowance for acceleration) .. .. 21·5 m.p.g.
Fuel tank capacity (maker's figure) 14 gals.

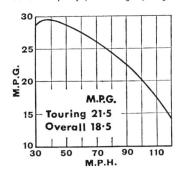

Pedal force for 20th stop 35
TEST 2. After top gear descent of steep hill falling approximately 600 ft. in ½ mile increase in brake pedal force for ½ g stop from 30 m.p.h.=nil.
Waterproofing
Increase in brake pedal force for ½ g stop from 30 m.p.h. after two runs through shallow watersplash at 30 m.p.h.=5 lb.

CLUTCH

Free pedal movement .. .. .. 1 in.
Additional movement to disengage clutch completely .. .. .. 4 in.
Maximum pedal load .. .. .. 45 lb.

STEERING

	ft.
Turning circle between kerbs:	
Left	35½
Right	38½
Turns of steering wheel from lock to lock	2¼
Steering wheel deflection for 50 ft. diameter circle	0·9 turns
Steering force (at rim of wheel) to move front wheels at rest ..	33 lb.

Steering force to hold car on 100 ft. diameter circle at 15 m.p.h. (=0·3 g approx.) .. .. 10½ lb.

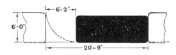

SPEEDOMETER

Speedometer at 30 m.p.h. ..	1½% fast
Speedometer at 60 m.p.h. ..	1¼% fast
Speedometer at 90 m.p.h. ..	2% fast
Speedometer at 120 m.p.h. ..	2½% fast
Distance recorder	accurate

WEIGHT

	cwt.
Kerb weight (unladen, but with oil, coolant and fuel for approximately 50 miles)	25·1
Front/rear distribution of kerb weight	49½/50½
Weight laden as tested	28·8

MOTOR week ending October 31 1964

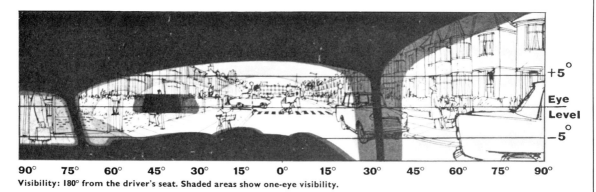

| 90° | 75° | 60° | 45° | 30° | 15° | 0° | 15° | 30° | 45° | 60° | 75° | 90° |

Visibility: 180° from the driver's seat. Shaded areas show one-eye visibility.

JAGUAR
E-type 4·2

Brakes

RETAINING the safety of twin master cylinders, the braking system now has a bigger servo which greatly reduces pedal effort. Our first E-type test car needed a 100 lb. push to record 0·96 g: 60 lb. is sufficient on the 4·2 for 0·97 g. There is also better progression and feel in the pedal, the disconcerting sponginess we recorded at low speeds before being completely absent in the latest car. A slight tendency to pull to one side marred high-speed stability under braking but otherwise the Dunlop discs on all four wheels felt immensely powerful and reassuring.

Although a severe Alpine test descent made the discs glow bright red, there was always plenty of braking in reserve to stop the car easily without snatch or unevenness, if at rather higher pedal pressures. So long as the brake fluid is in sound condition and of the right type, heat soak will not boil the hydraulics causing a complete loss of braking. This we confirmed after our standard brake fade test of 20 ½g stops at one minute intervals from the touring speed—a punishing 90 m.p.h. for the E-type. Pedal pressures increased a mere 10 lb and pedal travel was slightly longer towards the end of our test. Otherwise, the brakes were still true and very powerful—as we expected for Jaguar's own acceptance test is even more severe than ours at 30 stops from 100 m.p.h., again at one minute intervals.

The handbrake, working on the rear discs, is quite powerful and will hold on a 1-in-3 hill.

Comfort and control

THE E-TYPE belongs to the (happily) growing ranks of modern sports and GT cars in which outstanding handling has been combined with the ride of a comfortable saloon. There is none of the harsh, vertical bouncing that was once an inherent part of high performance cars, and even unexpectedly severe bumps taken at speed are smothered without unpleasant jarring, soft damping of the independent rear end reducing vertical movement. The structure feels immensely stiff, an impression strengthened by the way the whole car rides with any irregularities, like a block of wood in a stream, when travelling too slowly for the suspension to be wholly effective.

We found the entirely new bucket seats a big improvement on the old, especially now that deeper foot wells and greater seat movement (two modifications made some time ago) have greatly improved leg room for tall people. A small swivelling distance piece at the base of the folding squab gives two rake positions but most of our drivers would have liked to recline still further: the backrest is rather upright and tends to support the back at shoulder height rather than at the base of the spine unless you push well back into the

Unaltered bodily, the E-type retains the impressive lines of a classic GT. Wrap-round bumper and overriders protect the well finished paintwork, but the front air intake is still vulnerable to clumsy parkers (below).

The spare wheel is stowed beneath a large luggage platform which carries the boxes shown (total 7·2 cu. ft.) without obscuring the driver's visibility; the big rear door is released by a catch in the driver's side door pillar. A well-stocked tool kit lives with the spare wheel (bottom).

MOTOR week ending October 31 1964

soft, deep cushions. Even so, the driving position is generally good and one of our testers completed a one-day solo drive from Italy without any aches or discomfort.

An open throttle in the lower gears produces that characteristically hard, healthy snarl, yet cruising at 100 m.p.h. with the windows shut this is a particularly quiet and fussless car, wind and engine roar being unusually subdued. On a hot day sufficient cooling air can only be admitted through open side windows which disturb the quietness at speed. Better heat insulation round the gearbox and transmission tunnel have lessened the problem of overheating in the cockpit, but some form of cold air ventilation that by-passes the heater would still be a welcome refinement. Flaps above each foot well direct the heater's adequate output, two levers projecting from the passenger's side of the facia controlling the volume and temperature. Front hinged rear extractor windows can improve ventilation at the expense of some wind whistle.

Most drivers found the pendant pedals awkwardly placed for heel-and-toeing (curiously, they often are in sports cars), and both clutch and throttle have fairly long movements but very smooth and easy linkages. The gearlever—a short stick surmounted by a large round knob—is easily reached well forward on the massive transmission tunnel above which a glove box lid provides an arm rest without getting in the way.

Despite the low build and long bonnet literally bulging with power, the driver has a good view of the road immedi-

ately ahead and, except in busy town traffic, the projecting (invisible) ends and absence of an effective width gauge are of little handicap.

Tall people found the top edge of the large rear window (its effective size reduced by the slope) obscured any distant view through a mirror which itself can form a blind spot, mounted as it is in the centre of the screen. Shorter drivers did not find it troublesome.

New sealed beam lights improve dip and main beam intensity but it is still essential to keep the covers clean, for their acute slope exaggerates any film of bugs and dirt which high-speed motoring inevitably collects. On a very good road, we found the lights just good enough for 100 m.p.h., but generally they are inadequate for fast driving after dark.

Fittings and furniture

THE COCKPIT layout remains practically unchanged, with a comprehensive set of instruments set neatly into a padded facia panel, the large speedometer (reading to 160 m.p.h.) and rev counter being viewed through a three-spoke steering wheel. Some people thought the wooden rim would be easier to grip if it were a little thicker and it was slippery to hot hands. As in other Jaguars a row of identical minor switches are lined across the centre where they are easy to confuse (and locate) until the positions are memorized.

A very small facia cubbyhole is supplemented by a more useful lidded box on the central transmission tunnel, and a map/book shelf behind the seats. The large flat luggage platform, protected by metal strips with plastic inserts, can be reached through the rear door which opens well out of the way and is secured by a chrome stay. The forward edge of the platform hinges upwards to prevent luggage from sliding forward under braking. Like the outside door handles, petrol filler hole and central bonnet release, the rear door release is irritatingly small for man-sized hands.

Excellent handling and roadholding are the E-type's best concessions to safety. Inside, the projecting heater controls on the passenger's side are potentially dangerous but comfortable seat belts fitted to our test car minimized any risk of being thrown forward.

I, front suspension. 2, heater. 3, windscreen washer bottle. 4, alternator. 5, oil filler cap. 6, radiator cap. 7, coil. 8, distributor (far side of engine). 9, SU carburetter (one of three). 10, clutch and brake fluid reservoirs. II, oil dip stick. The raised bonnet restricts headroom (especially at the front) but accessibility is generally excellent.

MAKE Jaguar ● MODEL 4·2-litre E-type ● MAKERS Jaguar Cars Ltd., Coventry, England

ENGINE

Cylinders	6
Bore and stroke	92·07 mm. × 106 mm.
Cubic capacity	4,235 c.c.
Valves	Twin o.h.c.
Compression ratio	9 : 1 (8 : 1 optional)
Carburetter(s)	Three S.U. HD8
Fuel pump	S.U. AUF 301 electric
Oil filter	Tecalemit full flow
Max. power (gross)	265 b.h.p. at 5,400 r.p.m.
Max. torque (gross)	283 lb. ft. at 4,000 r.p.m.

TRANSMISSION

Clutch	Laycock Haüsserman 10 in. diameter diaphragm
Top gear (s/m)	1 : 1
3rd gear (s/m)	1·27 : 1
2nd gear (s/m)	1·74 : 1
1st gear (s/m)	2·68 : 1
Reverse	3·08 : 1
Final drive	Hypoid bevel with limited slip diff., 3·07 : 1

M.p.h. at 1,000 r.p.m. in:—
Top gear	24·4
3rd gear	19·4
2nd gear	14·05
1st gear	9·1

CHASSIS

Construction	Monocoque with space sub frame at front

BRAKES

Type	Dunlop discs with servo assistance
Dimensions	11 in. diameter front, 10 in. diameter rear
Friction areas	461 sq. in. rubbed area

SUSPENSION AND STEERING

Front	Independent by wishbones and torsion bars
Rear	Independent by lower wishbones with radius arm and twin coil springs; upper location by half shafts
Shock absorbers:	
Front and rear	Girling telescopic
Steering gear	Alford and Alder rack and pinion
Tyres	Dunlop RS5 6·40—15 with tubes

COACHWORK AND EQUIPMENT

Starting handle	No
Jack	Screw pillar
Jacking points	One each side
Battery	12 volt under bonnet

No. of electrical fuses	8
Indicators	Self-cancelling winkers
Screen wipers	Self-parking 2-speed electric with three blades
Screen washers	Twin jet electric
Sun visors	Two
Locks:	
With ignition key	Both doors
Interior heater	Fresh air system with temperature, volume and distribution controls
Upholstery	Leather
Floor covering	Pile carpet over felt
Alternative body types	Open two-seater

MAINTENANCE

Sump	15 pints S.A.E. 30
Gearbox	2½ pints S.A.E. 30
Rear axle	2½ pints S.A.E. 90 EP
Steering gear	Multi purpose grease
Cooling system	32 pints (2 drain taps)
Chassis lubrication	Every 2,500 miles to 6 points (additionally, 6 more at 5,000 and 2 more at 10,000)
Ignition timing	
Contact breaker gap	0·014–0·016 in.
Sparking plug type	Champion N5
Sparking plug gap	0·025 in.
Tappet clearances (cold)	Inlet 0·004 in., Exhaust 0·006 in.
Front wheel toe-in	1/16 – 1/8 in.
Castor angle	1½ ± ½°
Tyre pressures	23/30 p.s.i. for normal driving, 30/35 for sustained fast driving

AUTO TEST

JAGUAR E-TYPE V12 ROADSTER

More new wine in old bottle

AT-A-GLANCE: Considerable improvement in stowage space inside roadster based on long-wheelbase coupé body. Superbly smooth and tractable with refined V12 engine. Excellent braking, roadholding and ride. Poor minor controls, and only marginally improved ventilation from floor-level fresh air venting. Excellent hood marred by revised attachments. As ever, remarkable value for money.

IT is now some 20 months since we published the first road test of the Series III V12 E-Type in fixed-head coupé form. In the intervening months, we have been running a Roadster version long term, and it is this car that is the subject of this Autotest. In the time that the car has been in our possession, it has never ceased to be amongst the most coveted cars on the test fleet, and all have been unanimous in their praise for its most excellent qualities. The extended nature of this road test has given the very best opportunity to assess in great detail how the car stands up, and how it can be lived with as a sole means of transport, and it has been found lacking in only a few respects.

There is a very distinct paucity of open sports cars on the British market at this time. With the disappearance from this market of Ferrari (apart from the Dino Spider), Maserati and Aston Martin, the choice has narrowed down considerably. It has fallen, therefore, to Jaguar to uphold the honour of the quality open-top sports car and the E-Type in its latest form sets an undeniably high standard in this shrinking field. The American Federal regulations may well banish fully open cars forever, but in the meantime, it is still very pleasant to be able to appreciate the joys of open-air motoring in considerable luxury in the E-Type.

There are some people, no doubt, who still believe the sports cars should have a bone-hard ride, a glorious exhaust note and a draughty hood on a frame constructed from a multitude of sticks. To them the V12 Roadster would be a terrible disappointment, for in all these departments the car is highly refined, and in no way can using the car be considered an adventure in the traditional sports car idiom.

Despite an increase in cubic capacity over

the years of more than 40 per cent, the ultimate performance of E-Types has changed very little. This is due in part to a steady increase in overall weight, the current car being no less than 22 per cent heavier than it was at the beginning. Very little of this increase can be put down to the V12 engine, because it is largely made from aluminium alloy and in fact weighs only 65lb more than the cast-iron XK series six. Most of the extra must be attributed to a steady increase in weight of the furnishings and equipment more apposite to the role that the car now occupies. It was logical that the Roadster V12 should share the long-wheelbase chassis of the coupé and this certainly provides a welcome increase in the amount of interior stowage space. Opinions are bound to differ as to whether the car now looks too long in its "hood-down" form, but the continuing admiration of the passer-by is just as evident, so there cannot be a great deal wrong with the appearance.

Left: The superb view out over the curvaceous bonnet is as stirring as ever although the central bulge is no longer required
Above: Access to the massive engine is good, thanks to the forward-pivotted bonnet which is now supported by a gas strut on each side. Gaitering around the wheel wells helps to keep the bonnet area clean

Performance

As with the last three E-Types we have tested, the V12 Roadster ran at all times on its standard road tyres and the performance that we achieved should therefore be representative of that which any owner should be able to achieve. For the maximum speed runs and for continuous speeds in excess of 120 mph, the tyre pressures were increased to the recommended figure of 40 psi. At this pressure, the ride is extremely harsh at lower speeds and one is therefore faced with a dilemma on a journey containing both fast and slow sections. It is probably best to put up with the harshness at low speed rather than restrict cruising speeds when the conditions allow. When achieving its maximum of 143 mph, the engine was revving 6,200 rpm, which is well over the 5,750-rpm peak of the power curve and it is thus unlikely that a favourable downgrade would enable this figure

AUTOCAR 5 July 1973

Super Profile

JAGUAR E-TYPE V12 ROADSTER (5,343c.c.)

ACCELERATION

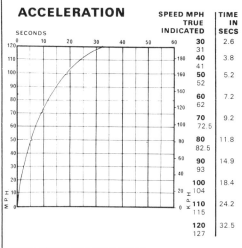

SPEED MPH TRUE INDICATED	TIME IN SECS
30 / 31	2.6
40 / 41	3.8
50 / 52	5.2
60 / 62	7.2
70 / 72.5	9.2
80 / 82.5	11.8
90 / 93	14.9
100 / 104	18.4
110 / 115	24.2
120 / 127	32.5

GEAR RATIOS AND TIME IN SEC

mph	Top (3.31)	3rd (4.60)	2nd (6.31)
10-30	6.7	4.4	3.2
20-40	5.8	3.7	2.9
30-50	5.4	3.7	2.8
40-60	5.4	3.7	3.0
50-70	5.4	3.8	3.5
60-80	5.4	4.3	4.5
70-90	5.9	5.0	—
80-100	6.8	6.3	—
90-110	8.8	9.0	—
100-120	15.3	—	—

Standing ¼-mile
15.1 sec 92 mph
Standing Kilometre
27.5 sec 116 mph
Test distance
3.970 miles
Mileage recorder
1.3 per cent over-reading

PERFORMANCE

MAXIMUM SPEEDS

Gear	mph	kph	rpm
Top (mean)	143	230	6,200
(best)	143	230	6,200
3rd	108	174	6,500
2nd	78	126	6,500
1st	52	84	6,500

BRAKES

FADE
(from 70 mph in neutral)
Pedal load for 0.5g stops in lb.

1	32	6	23
2	27	7	25
3	23	8	23
4	23	9	22
5	23	10	23

RESPONSE
(from 30 mph in neutral)

Load	g	Distance
20lb	0.26	116ft
40lb	0.48	63ft
60lb	0.88	34ft
70lb	1.04	29ft
Handbrake	0.28	108ft

Max. Gradient 1 in 3.

CLUTCH
Pedal 43lb and 6.5 in.

COMPARISONS

MAXIMUM SPEED MPH

Jaguar E-Type V12 Roadster	(£3,711)	**143**
A.C. 428 (Automatic)	(£6,914)	142
Porsche 911E Targa	(£6,020)	139
Mercedes-Benz 350SLCC (Auto)	(£6,798)	126
Triumph Stag	(£2,436)	116

0-60 MPH, SEC

A.C. 428	6.2
Porsche 911E Targa	6.4
Jaguar E-Type V12 Roadster	**7.2**
Mercedes-Benx 350SLCC	9.3
Triumph Stag	9.3

STANDING ¼-MILE, SEC

A.C. 428	14.2
Porsche 911E Targa	14.4
Jaguar E-Type V12 Roadster	**15.1**
Mercedes-Benz 350SLCC	17.0
Triumph Stag	17.1

OVERALL MPG

Triumph Stag	20.7
A.C. 428	17.0
Porsche 911E Targa	17.0
Jaguar E-Type V12 Roadster	**15.0**
Mercedes-Benz 350SLCC	15.0

GEARING
(with E70 VR15 in. tyres)

Top	23.0 mph per 1,000rpm
3rd	16.6 mph per 1,000rpm
2nd	12.2 mph per 1,000rpm
1st	7.8 mph per 1,000rpm

CONSUMPTION

FUEL
(At constant speed — mpg)

30 mph	22.2
40 mph	22.2
50 mph	22.0
60 mph	20.4
70 mph	18.4
80 mph	16.9
90 mph	15.8
100 mph	14.4

Typical mpg 16 (17.7 litres/100km)
Calculated (DIN) mpg 16.7 (16.9 litres/100km)
Overall mpg 15.0 (18.9 litres/100km)
Grade of fuel Premium 4-star (min. 97 RM)

OIL
Consumption (SAE 20W-50) 530 m.p.p.

TEST CONDITIONS:
Weather: Clear Wind: 0-8 mph
Temperature: 24 deg.C. (76 deg. F).
Barometer: 29.8 in. hg. Humidity: 48 percent.
Surfaces: dry concrete and asphalt.

WEIGHT:
Kerb Weight 29.5 cwt (3.316 lb-1,505 kg)
(with oil, water and half full fuel tank).
Distribution, per cent F. 51.1; R. 48.9.
Laden as tested: 32.7 cwt (3.662 lb-1,660kg)

TURNING CIRCLES:
Between kerbs L. 36 ft 4 in.; R. 35 ft 3 in.
Between walls L. 38 ft 0 in.; R. 36 ft 11 in.
Steering wheel turns. lock to lock 3.5.
Figures taken at 10,700 miles by our own
staff at the Motor Industry Research
Association proving ground at Nuneaton
and on the Continent.

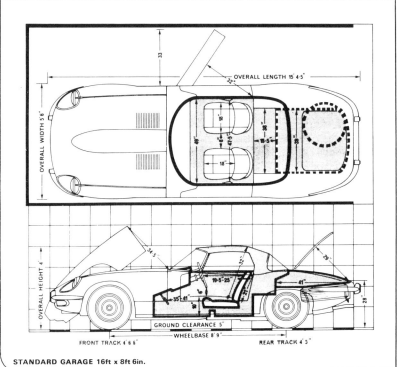

STANDARD GARAGE 16ft x 8ft 6in.

AUTOCAR 5 July 1973

SPECIFICATION — FRONT ENGINE, REAR-WHEEL DRIVE

ENGINE
Cylinders	12, in 60 deg vee
Main bearings	7
Cooling system	Water, twin electric fans and thermostat
Bore	90mm (3.54in.)
Stroke	70mm (2.76in.)
Displacement	5,343 c.c. (326 cu.in.)
Valve gear	Chain-driven single direct acting camshaft per cylinder bank
Compression ratio	9.0-1. Min. octane rating: 98RM
Carburettors	4 Stromberg 175 CD SE
Fuel pump	S.U. AUF 411
Oil filter	Full flow, paper element
Max. power	266 bhp (DIN) at 5,750 rpm
Max. torque	304 lb. ft. (DIN) at 3,500 rpm

TRANSMISSION
Clutch Type	Borg and Beck single dry plate diaphragm spring 10.5 in. dia.
Gearbox	4-speed all-synchromesh
Gear ratios	Top 1.0
	Third 1.389
	Second 1.905
	First 2.933
	Reverse 3.378
Final drive	Salisbury Powr-Lok limited-slip hypoid bevel, ratio 3.31:1

CHASSIS and BODY
Construction	Steel; monocoque centre section with tubular front sub-frame

SUSPENSION
Front	Independent; double wishbones, torsion bars, telescopic dampers, anti-roll bar
Rear	Independent; fixed-length drive-shafts lower wishbones, radius arms, coil springs containing telescopic dampers, anti-roll bar

STEERING
Type	Adwest, power-assisted rack and pinion
Wheel dia.	15.0 in.

BRAKES
Make and type	Girling. discs front and rear, ventilated at front
Servo	Girling Supavac "100"
Dimensions	F 11.18 in. dia.
	R 10.38 in. dia.
Swept area	F 234.5 sq. in., R 213.7 sq. in.
	Total 448.2 sq. in. (274 sq. in./ton laden)

WHEELS
Type	Ventilated steel disc
	6in. wide rim
Tyres — make	Dunlop SP Sport
— type	radial ply/tubeless
— size	E70 VR15in

EQUIPMENT
Battery	12 Volt 68 Ah. at 20 hr. rate
Alternator	60 amp./d.c.
Headlamps	Cibie Biode 220/110 watt (total) (on test car)
Reversing lamp	Standard
Electric fuses	8
Screen wipers	2-speed
Screen washer	Standard
Interior heater	Standard
Heated backlight	Not available
Safety belts	Extra
Interior trim	Leather facings on seats; pvc hood, lined
Floor covering	Deep pile nylon
Jack	Screw scissor type
Jacking points	Two each side beneath sill
Windscreen	Laminated
Underbody protection	Bitumastic overall

MAINTENANCE
Fuel tank	18.0 Imp. gallons (81.8 litres)
Cooling system	36.0 pints (20.5 litres)
Engine sump	19.0 pints (10.7 litres) SAE 20W-50 Change oil every 3,000 miles. Change filter every 6,000 miles.
Gearbox	3.0 pints. SAE 90 EP. Change every 12,000 miles
Final drive	2.75 pints. SAE 90 EP. Change every 12,000 miles
Grease	17 points every 6,000 miles. 4 wheel bearings every 12,000 miles
Valve clearance	Inlet 0.012/14 in. (cold) Exhaust 0.012/14 in. (cold)
Contact breaker	Fixed gap
Ignition timing	12 deg. BTDC (static) 4 deg. ATDC (stroboscopic at 700 rpm)
Spark plug	Type: Champion N10Y. Gap 0.025 in.
Compression pressure	120-140 psi
Tyre pressures	F 24; R 28 psi (normal driving) F 40; R 40 psi (high speed) F 40; R 40 psi (full load)
Max. payload	408 lb (185 kg)

Service Interval	3,000 miles	6,000 miles	12,000 miles
Time Allowed (hours and mins.)	1 — 30	4 — 30	4 — 45
Cost @ £3.30 per hour	£4.95	£14.85	£15.68
Oil Change	£3.90	£4.00	£4.00
Oil Filter	—	£0.54	£0.54
Air Filter	—	—	£1.37
Sparking plugs	—	—	£3.84
Total Cost:	**£8.85**	**£19.39**	**£25.43**

Routine Replacements:	Time hr min	Cost (labour)	Spares	TOTAL
Brake Pads	0 — 55	£3.02	£10.04	£13.06
Exhaust System	0 — 25	£1.38	£58.80	£60.18
Clutch	6 — 10	£20.13	£27.45	£47.58
Dampers — front	0 — 25	£1.38	£11.99	£13.37
Dampers — rear	2 — 10	£6.93	£18.04	£24.97
Replace Drive Shaft	1 — 30	£4.95	£15.61	£20.56
Replace Generator	1 — 00	£3.30	£51.81	£55.11
Replace Starter	0 — 55	£3.02	£47.79	£50.81

to be exceeded by very much. At this speed, which the car held without temperament for several miles, the combination of tyre and wind roar is very high, although the car felt rock-steady. Jaguar do not recommend that engine speeds exceeding 6,000 rpm be held for extended periods and a maximum of 135 mph at 6,000 rpm will be the more usual attainment. Perhaps more important than outright maximum is the ability of the car to cruise effortlessly all day at between 120 and 130 mph. At this speed tyre roar is less, and wind roar is also more subdued. During its stay with us, the V12 was used on a trip to Sicily and it is on this sort of Continental journey that the car comes into its own. The ability to put over 700 miles into each day puts even the most distant of overseas resorts within easy reach, and allows the maximum time to be spent at the destination.

In our road test of the V12 coupé, we thought that the standard 3.31-to-1 final drive ratio would enable an improvement to be made on the acceleration figures taken with the optional 3.07-to-1 ratio. The V12 Roadster was delivered with the standard axle and it was therefore a considerable disappointment to find that the acceleration is, in fact, not as good as that of the coupé. The two cars have similar laden weights, and it is unlikely that any possible aerodynamic advantage of the coupé could account for the differences. It is more likely that the usual slight variation between two cars from the same production line is present. Any owner should, therefore, at least have a car of similar performance to the test car, if not one that is slightly faster. The coupé that was tested proved capable of reaching 100 mph from rest in 16.4 sec, while the Roadster was exactly 2 sec slower.

The difference between the two cars is most marked at the top end of the power curve. Although the coupé is, for instance, slower from 20 to 40 mph in second gear, it is appreciably quicker from 50 to 70 mph in the same gear.

However, these differences apart, the performance of the Roadster is impressive by any standards. Any car that takes less than 6 seconds for each 20 mph increment from 20 to 90 is very fast, and the smooth ease with which the Jaguar does this is most impressive. While taking the acceleration figures for the car, an experiment was tried using only 4,000 rpm in each gear, and it was found that the car was less than 1 sec slower from rest to 100 mph than it had been using up to 6,000 rpm in each gear. As a further demonstration of the remarkable flexibility of the engine, the V12 proved capable of accelerating from rest to 110 mph in top gear in 36.4 sec. In practice this means that very rapid progress can be made without continuous use of the gearbox and this contributes considerably to one's relaxed enjoyment of the car.

The deceptively smooth way in which the power is delivered, and the low level of noise except at very high speeds, mean that it is an easy car in which to misjudge speeds. There is little increase in exhaust noise and even with the hood down, in a narrow high-walled street the most one hears is a pleasant musical hum from the exhaust. There is very little whine from the camshaft chains but at very high revs with the hood down an excited chatter, rising to a deep-throated thrum, can be heard from the valve-gear. At no time can any induction roar be discerned.

The turbine-like smoothness with which the engine provides a sustained shove in the back is almost uncanny, the more so when one accelerates hard in top gear without even a gear change to interrupt one's headlong dash into the distance.

It is perhaps as well that limited use need

AUTOTEST JAGUAR E-TYPE V12 ROADSTER . . .

be made of the gearbox, for although the all-synchromesh unit that was introduced in 1964 works well, the change is not particularly quick, and the movement between gears is long. Sometimes there is baulking when selecting bottom gear and some increase in effort is noticeable when the unit is very hot. With such a wide span of torque, the choice of ratios need not be so critical; those chosen suit the engine admirably and provide a good overlap of performance in each gear. The busy noise of 12 cylinders can lead one to think that the car is too low-geared, and there is even a temptation to change up when already in top gear.

Despite its advanced design, the engine is not as efficient in terms of fuel economy as the old XK series, and even the most careful use of the accelerator will not give better than 16 to 17 mpg. To date, our car has returned an overall of 15.0 mpg, and while this includes a high proportion of London commuting, checks on other cross-country journeys show that a typical figure of around 16.0 mpg should be expected. On the 4,000 mile trip to Sicily and back, consumption worked out at 15.6 mpg and since this journey included a variety of different road conditions, it may be considered as typical.

Octane requirements for the engine are only 97, and no trouble has been experienced with either British 4-star or the various super premium fuels available on the Continent. The range provided by the 18-gallon tank is therefore between 200 and 250 miles, which means a stop every 2½ to 3 hours. There is a fuel low-level warning tell-tale that starts to flash when there are about six gallons remaining, and the light shines continuously when down to the last three gallons. The tank will take the full rate of delivery from all pumps, although its flat shape means that the last gallon needs to be handled carefully.

Ride and Handling

For those who continue to feel that power-steering means a lack of feel and precision, the Series III E-Type is something of an eye-opener. The amount of assistance provided is just right for relieving the tedium of parking or low speed manoeuvring, while at speed, stability and precision are excellent. One or two of our more sensitive drivers thought the initial repsonse a little too abrupt and wondered if some more castor angle would improve the feel overall. As it stands the power assistance has enabled a small steering wheel to be adopted, and this can be twirled with a delightful absence of effort when negotiating roundabouts or tight bends alike. Response is quick, and road shocks are well insulated.

The high tyre pressures required for speeds in excess of 120 mph affect the stability to a limited extent by introducing a tendency to swing slightly between power on and power off conditions. From our experience of the V12 coupé it has been found that the introduction of a small front-rear differential can assist in reducing this. At town speeds there is some harshness and bump-thump from the tyres, and this increases considerably if the high-speed pressures are maintained. Dropping the pressures to the recommended 24 psi front, 28 psi rear not only reduces the harshness, but also improves the stability.

The considerable weight is almost perfectly distributed 50:50 and the car feels extremely

well balanced. Such balance when allied to the superb grip of the Dunlop SP Sport tyres means that it is extremely difficult to break adhesion at either end of the car. There is very little trace of roll, and under most conditions, the car just goes where it is pointed. In the wet, the grip is also excellent, but some caution must be exercised on really slippery roads, as the engine pours out its considerable torque so smoothly that wheelspin can occur at remarkably low revs. Anti-dive characteristics have been introduced into the front suspension, and this effectively limits dipping of the nose under heavy braking. Among the advantages that arise from the lack of nose dip is that at night, one does not lose any of the effective light from the headlamps, and faster progress can be made after dark as a result.

The brakes were perhaps the poorest feature of both the Series I and Series II E-Types, but those on the Series III V12 are beyond criticism. Response and anti-fade characteristics are as one would hope for in a car of this nature, and the effort required for check braking is pleasantly light without in any way lacking progression. The ventilated discs at the front are occasionally guilty of producing some subdued groans, but this in no way affects their efficiency. The car is capable of producing a

better than 1g stop with only 70 lb pedal effort, and the brakes now bite well at low speeds which should help to reduce the number of E-Types with minor bumps and bruises on their long snouts.

The handbrake is effective, but requires a great deal of effort to produce results. That on the test car has a longer lever than on earlier models, but two hands are needed to release it when the maximum travel has been used on a steep incline.

Fittings and Furniture

As we were forced to say in the case of the coupé V12, it really is a shame that the opportunity has not been taken to improve the controls and interior fitments with the Series III car. Since we tested the coupé, footwell vents have been added, and they do a little to improve matters, but the primitive water valve temperatue control remains, and the lack of face level ventilation is a considerable disadvantage. The problem is compounded by the amount of heat that is radiated from the very large engine. Despite copious asbestos shielding, much heat still penetrates to the passenger compartment, and once the ram effect is lost as one slows down, the interior of

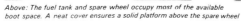

Above: The fuel tank and spare wheel occupy most of the available boot space. A neat cover ensures a solid platform above the spare wheel

Above: The boot is shallow, but a large suitcase can be carried provided that it is positioned in the centre and to the back of the space, and flexible hand baggage can then be stowed around the sides and end of the suitcase.

Super Profile

AUTOCAR 5 July 1973

the car can become uncomfortably hot. Control of the heater distribution is also crude, with just small, illegibly-marked thumb wheels on the facia, and an inaccessible control for the driver's side beneath the facia.

The seats are comfortable and the control of rake is adequately fine, but the leather wearing surfaces tend to become shiny and slippery with age, and as the passenger toe-board is right down into the footwell, the passenger tends to submarine under the seatbelt on a journey. Regular application of saddle soap or similar would help to alleviate the hardening of the leather surface.

The Kangol seatbelts are easy to put on as they now have a single handed fastening arrangement. If the optional head restraints are fitted, they catch the belt in their lowest position and prevent the inertia reel from retracting.

Much valuable room has been gained behind the seats by the use of the long-wheelbase chassis, and the space above the differential nose is now filled in by a useful locker that runs the full width of the car. The lid of this locker folds neatly in two, and a surprising amount of oddments of different shape and size can be hidden from view inside. In the closed position, this locker forms a wide, flat shelf on which

Below: The adoption of the long-wheelbase chassis of the 2 + 2 coupe has provided a welcome increase in interior stowage space. There is a large locker above the differential, whose lid forms a useful shelf in its down position. Care must be exercised to ensure that luggage on the rear shelf does not obstruct the inertia reel seat belts

further gear can be placed, and where, at a pinch, a small child can be carried for short trips.

The seating position is good, with the full complement of instruments laid out in front of the driver and on his left. The steering column is adjustable for reach, and the seat adjustment is generous. Power steering enables a small diameter steering wheel to be used, and this no longer interferes with the knees, as it did on earlier models. The confusing row of rocker switches beneath the supplementary instruments continues, however, and although there is a multi-position stalk to the right of the steering wheel, it does not control the windscreen washing and wiping, whose controls are among the row of switches on the facia. Headlamp dipping is controlled by a hand dipswitch to the right of the steering wheel which is annoying just out of fingertip reach with one's hand on the wheel.

To the left of the facia, there is a lockable glove compartment, which is just not deep enough to take a conventional-sized camera. Between the two seats is a larger compartment with a padded lid, which is of a useful size for maps etc.; there are stowage shelves below both sides of the facia but their shallow openings fit them only for flat objects.

The adoption of the more steeply-sloped windscreen of the long-wheelbase Series II, has meant the disappearance of the three wiper setup, and the remaining two blades sweep the big screen well, leaving only two blind spots at the extreme edges of the screen, where it curves round to meet the side-windows. Visibility is good to the front and sides, although the rear quarters are blind when either the hood or the optional hard-top are in position. The dipping mirror gives good rearward vision, although when it is adjusted to give optimum field of vision for a tall driver, it obscures vision towards the kerb, and also of the road ahead when one is halfway round a right-angle left-hand bend. The test car was fitted with an outside mirror on the driver's door that is adjustable by a small "joystick" from inside the car; the only disadvantage of it being that it is jarred out of adjustment each time the door is slammed.

Following our experience of Cibié Biode headlamps on the previous coupé test car, these excellent lights were again specified on the Roadster. The halogen filaments and carefully controlled beam pattern, give excellent lighting at night, and the sharp cut-off obviates the need for fog lamps. There are twin reversing lamps that come on automatically when reverse is engaged, but their effectiveness is reduced by the amount of soot and dirt that collects on the rear panel on which they are positioned, and their glasses require frequent cleaning.

Living with the Jaguar V12 E-type

The price of £3,710.60 for the test car on the road, includes a number of extras all of which are desirable, but not all necessary. In its standard form, the car is fully equipped and the extras on the test car have added to this refinement. The hardtop is a most substantial and well finished affair, and two people are required to remove or replace it. In winter, it enables the car to revert to the role of closed coupé, and the built-in vents give air extraction that is lacking with the hood. With the hardtop on, the engine noise is further reduced, as it absorbs noise that the hood material cannot. The hood itself is well made, but not as simple to raise and lower as in the past. There are Velcro patches along the tops of the window seals and also at the base of the quarter panels and these can be used to tension the hood, and keep its neat appearance. It is

essential to release the two press studs at the outer sides of the hood, as, if the hood is lowered with them attached, the material will tear.

Most of the items requiring regular attention are readily accessible beneath the vast bonnet, the sinuous dipstick being particularly easy to reach. The radiator header tank is set well forward at the front of the engine bay, and it is quite a stretch across the top of the engine to reach it. The four carburettors sit well up at the top of the engine and are thus easy to work on. There are splash guards over the sets of ignition for each bank of cylinders to prevent water from penetrating through the bonnet louvres and onto the ignition.

Boot space is seriously curtailed by the wedge shape of the tail and by the necessity for such a large fuel tank. It is, however, possible to get at least one large suitcase into the boot and to pack small squashy "grips" and clothing around it. An unfortunate feature is that the boot hinges are very deep, and as the lid swings downwards, the hinges foul on anything stowed in their way. The spare wheel is housed beneath the boot floor, and everything must be removed from the boot in the event of a puncture.

Although the tank has an 18 gal capacity, the majority of this will be used in less than 3 hours on a long journey. One is then faced with putting in a further £7 worth, or nearly £9 worth on the Continent. It is obligatory, therefore to start a long journey with a full wallet or a widely-accepted credit card.

The limitations of the heating system have already been expressed, and it is sensible of Jaguar to make air conditioning available on Home market cars, for although the equipment is expensive at £242, it is the lack of adequate ventilation and cooling that more than any other adverse factor will cool one's enthusiasm for the car.

A look at the remaining competition will show how well the V12 Roadster fits into the high-performance bracket of refined sports cars. It can hold its own respectably on performance and costs appreciably less than all its rivals except the Triumph Stag, and as value for money it is as attractive as ever.

MANUFACTURER:
British Leyland — Jaguar Cars Limited, Browns Lane, Allesley, Coventry.

PRICES

Basic	£2,785.00
Car Tax	£232.00
VAT	£302.00
Total (in GB)	**£3,319.00**
Seat belts	£16.38
Licence	£25.00
Delivery charge (London)	£15.00
Number plates	£3.00
Total on the Road	
(exc. insurance)	**£3,378.38**
Insurance	Group 7

EXTRAS (inc. TAX)

*Remote control wing mirror	£5.96
*Radio with twin speakers and electric	
* aerial	£81.00
Air conditioning	£241.91
*Chrome plated pressed steel wheels	£51.60
*Hardtop in matching paint colour	£144.79
*Head restraints	£25.03
*Cibié Biode headlamps	£23.84
Chrome plated wire wheels	£103.20
Sundym glass	£15.79
*Fitted to test car	
TOTAL AS TESTED ON THE	
ROAD	**£3,710.60**

BUYING & OWNER'S VIEW

My own first E-type driving experience was in 1961, when Victors, the Ulster Jaguar distributors, let me take their new demonstrator around the famous Dundrod road circuit near Belfast. It was bright red and it seemed perfect in every way. I thought it a dream to drive, despite my familiarity with it in the development stage before I'd been called away from Coventry to do my National Service. (In fact, from the late 'fifties we'd often had a chance to examine the little prototype, E1A, at the apprentice hostel during test runs). More than twenty years later, while touring the dealerships to give talks on Jaguar's illustrious history, I came across that same red roadster in a Fife showroom. It gave me quite a thrill, not just to recognise the familiar machine with its side bonnet locks and other early production identifying marks, but to think that so many early E-types are now being restored to their former glory.

Like all Jaguars and indeed most other cars, E-types respond to sympathetic treatment, storage and maintenance. Leave them be, in the British climate at least, and they will soon need attention.

During a period at *Motoring News* followed by many years back with the old firm in Coventry, I got to know the ways of the E-type in its many and varied guises. Perhaps familiarity breeds practicality, but the opportunity to live so close to the car made it seem superfluous to own one; that really would have been a case of having one's cake and eating it. It is easy to see one's errors in hindsight; it is also easy to forget that £2000 was a great deal of money in the nineteen-sixties.

It is important, therefore, that I use this relatively small space to pass on some words of experience from today's owners, and where better to go than the E-type Register of the Jaguar Drivers' Club? — the officially-recognised association in the UK. (There are, of course, national motor clubs for Jaguar owners around the world).

The E-type's charisma is hard to put into words. Today's owners are, it seems, nearly all folk who dreamed beautiful dreams when the car was announced in 1961 but were too young or poor to buy. There are still races at JDC meetings in which E-types compete, but values have shot up and people with good vehicles have followed the example of their XK-owning predecessors and opted for the trials and tribulations of *concours d'élégance,* as opposed to the dangers of damage on the track. Mainly, though, it is as a road car that the E-type still excels.

George Gibbs was the first person I tackled about ownership. He has three Jaguars at the time of writing, all V12s — one being an XJ-S with the registration number 53 CAT. He *has* owned three E-types (a six and two twelves) and he spends virtually all his spare time carrying out his duties as chairman of the E-type Register and its competitions committee. How did he get involved with Jaguar?

"I know I'm a pretty typical case", says George Gibbs. "When I was younger, I used to stop almost daily at the local Jaguar showrooms in Derby and nose around. I saved hard, but my first Jaguar had to be a Mark Two saloon — a lovely car, but not the E of my dreams. That came later, when my family had begun to grow up sufficiently to allow me the fun of a 4.2 fixed-head. Perhaps it wasn't a practical thing to do; it became part of the family. I saw it not just as one of the world's engineering masterpieces but as an extension of my family and me. Every owner cherishes his or her E-type for one or other reason. I revered mine. It wasn't just a status symbol. Just ask an E-type owner how often he photographs his car? — and how often his family? I think an E-type is a man's best friend after his wife (... or before)". I noted that his last remark could be taken several ways, and switched to the question of purchase.

The Jaguar Drivers' Club is what it says it is: a club for people who really use their cars, and expect to keep them running. It likes to be of practical help. George Gibbs advises: "If at all possible, buy through a club member. Within the register committee, we are happy to offer advice. Experience in judging *concours* can also help the potential purchaser. There are plenty of books on 'Where The Rust Starts', but condition is a direct result of maintenance. I don't believe Jaguar ever made what people call a 'Friday Afternoon' car. I've known several good Es with well over 100,000 miles on the clock. I also know an under-40,000 late-model V12 so poorly cared-for that it needed many new body panels. The thing is: don't rush into purchasing a superficially-stunning E. Check with us at the club or, of course, get advice from the AA or RAC. It is such a fabulous car that the newcomer to the scene *could* let his or her heart rule the head".

There are certain preferences among the different six-cylinder E-types but, generally speaking, the two camps are the "sixes" and the "twelves". It is not a matter of the twain never meeting; the cars just seem to have their own special and entirely different characters. At Jaguar it was known from the late nineteen-sixties that a new 'GT' model was on its way; outside, rumours of the Jaguar 'F-type' were almost as rife. (The name 'XKF' was in fact approved at BL's headquarters in 1974, but the car was launched as the 'XJ-S' a year later). Of course there *was* no F-type Jaguar. At the time the 1971-75 V12 E-type looked very much a stopgap; ''new wine in an old bottle'' was a favourite but oversimplifying quote. In fact it was a remarkable machine. I spoke to the enthusiastic owners of many; and in each case the argument was compelling!

Gordon Skelton has a lovely 1965 metallic dark green 2-seater, fixed-head coupe — to my mind the most beautiful production E-type of all, and to his too! ''I was hooked on the six-cylinder E-type from the start. I had a 420 saloon and then a 3.8 XK150S before the E; I've still got the XK, which has virtually the same engine as the E-type. I learned to love Jaguars, *and* I learned to play it carefully when E-hunting. When mine was advertised in the West Country a few years ago I knew I was dealing with a genuine fellow. I don't like the roadster's buffeting or the 2+2's looks even with the later, less upright screen; the coupe is my ideal — in 'Series One' form, with the enclosed headlamps — and there's something special about the way it drives''.

The Gordon Skelton E-type has a known history (which it is *always* best to establish and to document if possible), and was bought with privately-fitted Tecalemit fuel injection. (Jaguar and Tecalemit did a lot of joint work in this field at one time.) The new owner had no difficulty in selling the equipment, as he wanted the car in original condition and specification. Some panel work was necessary, and this was done by a specialist — as was the provision of new upholstery by Carl Watson, one of several former Jaguar craftsmen who continue to ply their trade as freelances. ''I'd

recommend his work to anyone'', says Gordon Skelton. ''Word of mouth is the best means of sharing information, and by the same token I've learned of several other specialist services which aren't usually advertised. This is the greatest of all the Jaguar Drivers' Club's Register activities: members helping one another to keep our cars up to scratch. Parts? Well, P.J. Evans of Birmingham — in fact, I use their Redditch branch — are just about the oldest Jaguar agents anywhere, and I must say they often come up trumps with things I need for the XK and the E-type. They and other dealers have a helpful computer search system, so my advice would be: don't overlook the official Jaguar distributor and dealer channels''.

What about authenticity in restoration? Gordon Skelton takes a balanced view: ''I think it's much more important to keep a car as near original as possible than to overdo things; the E-type is a spectacular-looking machine anyway, and isn't improved by over-polishing and so on. The manifolds and camshaft covers and original gold-painted head look fine, as long as all the surrounding items that *were* black *stay* black! Incidentally, I know people are likely to query the black interior leather colour, but I have the original document which says that it was put in at the works for £10 extra, for the first owner''.

How does Gordon Skelton keep his car, which won the 1982 E-type Register 'Series 1' prize, in such consistently good condition? ''The dampness in this country can play havoc. One winter in an unheated garage, and the surface corrosion is everywhere; nowadays I leave a night storage heater close to each car, giving out just enough to keep the air reasonably dry and circulating. Even having said that, there is no substitute for hours and hours of dedication with the workshop manual at the ready and, preferably, a pit in the garage; it's not satisfactory to grovel under a

car. The pleasure of the resultant motoring is payment enough, to me''.

Gordon Skelton's love of the six-cylinder XK engine goes back to the 1960s, when he was thinking of buying a rather tatty XK140 at an auction. Could he hear the engine running, please? Of course, sir; it is, sir! (He stopped bidding at £150; it went for £160. Times change).

The V12 Jaguars are in a different world, in some ways at least. *Alan Hames* has had his car from new, in 1973; often a top prize-winner, his primrose yellow roadster is always immaculate. He started his Jaguar motoring with an earlier roadster (his preference is for open cars, with the optional hardtop). Then one day he parked it alongside one of the then-new Series Three E-types. He takes up the story: ''I fell for the new car at once. I liked the beefier appearance, the aggressive stance; tyres were broader by the 1970s, of course, and the flared wheelarches appealed to me. Much as I liked my six, it looked spindly, to me, alongside the Series Three. Besides that I'd always had a hankering for a V8-engined car; now there was a 'bargain' V12 on the market I simply had to have it''.

What about the complexities? ''Really, there are none'', says Alan Hames. ''That is — provided you don't fiddle! I had the four carburetters set accurately soon after I bought the car, because they needed setting; but they haven't needed setting since. The only change I've stuck to has been a different type of plug from standard, as the regular ones definitely caused uneven running''. (George Gibbs also lists plugs as an important 'peace-of-mind' item in connection with E-types. ''They go off-song quickly'', he says. ''Their engines run hot, and the plugs have a short life; keep plugs clean and change them often, the engine will sound sweeter and your mind will be eased''). The more modern and efficient fuel-injected V12 engine was never offered in the E-type;

and it is a complex job to modify the existing V12, although several people have done it. The car is, usually, considered too valuable in its standard form to be thus modified for road use.

Alan Hames is happy with the reliability, with certain provisos. "You need to be ready for water-pump failure", he says. "I think about four failed during the Jaguar Drivers' Club's E-type anniversary runs to Geneva. On the other hand, very little other trouble was experienced by anyone except, possibly, as a result of lack of normal servicing or preparation. In this context I must mention wheel bearings; E-type owners have discovered cases where there has been insufficient grease in the first place, the centrifugal force throwing the grease outwards far enough to let the bearings run dry. It's a standard thing to check as far as I'm concerned".

In a book of this kind, one can only scratch the surface of the problems and undoubted pleasures of E-type ownership. This is a collector's car and a popular one, so there is no shortage of first-hand and usually willing advice to be had by the inquisitive purchaser, even though personal judgement must be the arbiter in the end.

The final voice of experience here is that of *George Gibbs* once again: "Only the brake specialist is prepared to race seriously these days! The E-type is, however, an enjoyable sprint and hillclimb car, and the club will be happy to supply information on the opportunities. It is becoming difficult to justify using an E-type on a daily basis nowadays in view of the ever-increasing costs – but then ALL motoring is costly. In summing-up, I feel it is evident that as cars get older their owners find the support of a club more and more valuable. OK, so you can take short cuts, buy glassfibre bits, and keep your car running somehow, day to day. When you're ready to treat it as a classic, though, I can't see the wrong materials being a pleasing substitute; the other thing, of course, is to think seriously before embarking upon the many hours needed to do a proper restoration and maintenance job. It's always sad to see a project left undone because of lost interest. We don't make any recommendations, but we do note the good intentions of the Jaguar Specialists' Association. If in need of encouragement or guidance, consult them or, of course, ourselves – the E-type Register of the Jaguar Drivers' Club. Happy Jaguar motoring!"

CLUBS, SPECIALISTS & BOOKS

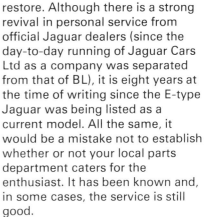

Clubs

The Jaguar Drivers' Club is well-established, having been factory-approved since 1956. Very soon after E-types became familiar on British roads (some time after the original announcement, due to export priority), an **E-type Register** was established within the club. Indeed all models of Jaguar are identifiable with one of the JDC's registers.

Membership of the JDC is virtually essential, if only to keep fully up to date with the advertisers of services and, from time to time, comments upon them through the monthly *Jaguar Driver* magazine. In it there is an E-type section which, as with all club publications, varies in quantity and quality depending upon the enthusiasm of the members to share their experiences with others. In the case of the E-type, the reader is well-served. The JDC's annual E-type Day is one of the club's major events, and there are more events (usually starting with a Silverstone race meeting in the spring) in the year than most people's diaries can cope with.

There *are* overseas JDC sections, but most countries with a good Jaguar population have their own national club. If you do not know how to make contact with it, the official Jaguar importer should

be able to tell you – or, failing that, the JDC headquarters should have the latest information.

North America has always been the biggest market for Jaguar cars, which is why there is a central office near New York City (at Leonia, just across the Washington Bridge) with the latest information on the different clubs across the nation.

These are the important starting points:

JDC (General Secretary),
Jaguar House,
18 Stuart Street,
Luton, LU1 2SL,
Bedfordshire,
England.
(tel: 0582 419332)

JDC E-type Register
(Sec., George Gibbs),
Burghclere Grange School,
Burghclere,
Newbury,
Berkshire,
England.

Jaguar Clubs of N.America
(Co-ordinator),
600 Willow Tree Road,
Leonia,
New Jersey 07605, USA.

Specialists

Good E-types fetch good money, and so bad E-types are costly to

restore. Although there is a strong revival in personal service from official Jaguar dealers (since the day-to-day running of Jaguar Cars Ltd as a company was separated from that of BL), it is eight years at the time of writing since the E-type Jaguar was being listed as a current model. All the same, it would be a mistake not to establish whether or not your local parts department caters for the enthusiast. It has been known and, in some cases, the service is still good.

Because so many small firms have offered their unofficial services in recent years, and because some of them have created a number of unhappy customers for a whole variety of reasons, an organisation called the **Jaguar Specialists' Association** was formed in the early 1980s.

The JSA seems to be working well in its endeavours to give the Jaguar name as good a reputation in the 'enthusiast' trade as it has regained in new-car quality. The association's members cover most aspects of restoration – mechanical work, coachbuilding and panel work, spares and service – and are the sort of folk who will take time to talk to you on the 'phone or when you call in on them. Jaguar involvement is an infectious enthusiasm.

Jaguar Cars Ltd and the JDC stand apart from any comments and recommendations, but word of mouth soon gets around. The companies on this page are the JSA members in early 1983. Non-membership is NO STIGMA WHATSOEVER, and several firms preferring to go it entirely alone are known to have done excellent work. JSA membership helps the line to be drawn for the purpose of this listing. Besides the *Jaguar Driver* magazine, all the sporting or historic motoring periodicals carry advertisements placed by Jaguar 'specialists'. To find out who is a specialist in what, however, there is no substitute for personally going and looking!

British Sports Car Centre Ltd.,
299-309 Goldhawk Road,
London. W12, England.
Tel: 01-748 7823/7824
Spares.

Roger Bywater Engineering Ltd.,
Unit 4, Hillgate Ind. Estate,
Carrington Field Street,
Stockport,
Cheshire. SK1 3JN, England.
Proprietor: R. Bywater
Tel: 061-480 4870
Mechanical repairs, fuel injection.

Classic Autos,
10 High Street,
Kings Langley,
Hertfordshire, England.
Proprietor: A. Finburgh
Tel: Kings Langley (09277) 62994
Body repairs, panel manufacturing

Classic Power Units,
Tile Hill, 18 Trevor Close,
Coventry, England.
Proprietor: G. Hodge
Tel: Coventry (0203) 461136
Engine rebuilds & servicing.

D.K. Engineering,
10/16 Hallwell Road,
Northwood,
Middlesex, England.
Proprietor: D. Cottingham
Tel: Northwood (09274) 21399
Renovations, mechanical rebuilds.

Coventry Auto Components,
Gillingwood,
Waste Lane,
Berkswell,
Nr. Coventry, Warwickshire,
England.
Proprietor: T. Worthington
Tel: Coventry (0203) 464644
Spares.

Deetype Replicas Ltd.,
South Gibcracks Farm,
Bicknacre Road,
East Hanningfield,
Chelmsford,
Essex. CM3 5AP, England.
Proprietor: B. Wingfield
Tel: Chelmsford (0245) 415380
Copies of D-Types & C-Types +
design.

Forward Engineering Ltd.,
Barston Lane,
Barston,
Solihull,
West Midlands. B92 0JP, England.
Proprietor: R.T. Beaty
Tel: Hampton-in-Arden (06755)
2163/2530
Engine development, exchange
engines, servicing etc.

Alan R. George,
Plot 11,
Small Firms Compound,
Dodwells Bridge Ind. Estate,
Hinckley, Leicester, England.
Proprietor: A. George
Tel: Hinckley (0455) 615937
Manual & auto transmissions.

A.W. Hannah,
Central Garage,
Snaith, near Goole,
Humberside, England.
Proprietor: A. Hannah
Tel: Goole (0405) 860321
Service, repairs, restoration.

Bill Lawrence Esq.,
9 Badgers Walk,
Dibden Purlieu,
Hampshire, England.
Proprietor: W. Lawrence
Tel: Hythe (0703) 846768
Panel manufacturing.

Lynx Engineering,
Castleham Ind. Estate,
St. Leonards-on-Sea,
East Sussex. TN38 9NR, England.
Proprietor: G. Black
Tel: Hastings (0424) 51277

Total restoration, mechanical &
body manufacture of sports cars.

Phillips Garage
103/7 New Canal Street,
Digbeth,
Birmingham. B5 5RA, England.
Proprietor: H. Phillips
Tel: 021-643 0912
Mechanical repairs, exchange
engines, servicing etc.

R.S. Panels,
Kelsey Close,
Attleborough Fields Ind. Estate,
Nuneaton. CV11 6RS, England.
Proprietor: R. Smith
Tel: Nuneaton (0203)
388572/89561
Body rebuilds, manufacture of
panels & complete bodies.

S.S. & Classic Restoration,
Cemere Green Farm,
Cemere Green,
Pulham Markets,
Diss,
Norfolk, England.
Proprietor: D. Barber
Tel: Diss (0379) 74361
Spares & restoration, pre-XK.

S.S. & L. Automobile Engineers,
Homefarm,
Holmlea Road,
Datchet,
Berkshire, England.
Proprietor: M. Sherwin
Tel: Slough (0753) 47016
Mechanical repairs.

Suffolk & Turley,
Unit 7,
Attleborough Fields Ind. Estate,
Garrett Street,
Nuneaton,
Warwickshire, England.
Proprietors: E. Suffolk & M. Turley
Tel: Nuneaton (0203) 381429
Trim.

Swallow Engineering,
6 Gibcracks,
Basildon,
Essex, England.
Tel: Basildon (0268) 558418
Restoration, body & mechanical
rebuilds.

Books

In a way, the E-type enthusiast is spoilt for choice as regards literature.

As distinct from the factory manual, Haynes, the publishers of this *Super Profile,* offer their own Owners Workshop Manual. The point about Haynes manuals is that they are all done from 'ground up' experience – no plagiarism here! Proprietor John Haynes is a Jaguar enthusiast himself which, perhaps, accounts for the Jaguar titles on his shelves. The standard work of historical reference – putting the E-type into perspective – is Paul Skilleter's prize-winning *Jaguar Sports Cars* (Foulis/Haynes) – a massive work in the 'labour of love' category. The same author has done a much more compact book on the E-type alone, which includes such useful chapter headings as 'Buying an E-type' and 'Spares and Maintenance', the title being *The Jaguar E-Type, A Collector's Guide*

(Motor Racing Publications). A sparklier, more subjective book is Chris Harvey's *E-Type, The End Of An Era,* (Oxford Illustrated Press/Haynes).

1984 should see the publication of my own book by Foulis/Haynes: *Jaguar – Sports Racing and Works Competition Cars since 1954.* It will include the story of the D-type, the lightweight E-type and of course the V12 E-type racing effort in the USA in the mid-1970s, leading to the revival of Jaguar's interest in racing in 1982 and 1983.

Brooklands Books provide a useful compilation of contemporary articles, descriptions, and road-test reports in softback form. For the history of the company and its

people, Lord Montagu's *Jaguar, A Biography* (Quiller Press) and my own *Jaguar, The History Of a Great British Car* (Patrick Stephens) are the alternatives. For a purely personal and most enjoyable account of E-type ownership, Denis Jenkinson's *Jaguar E-Type Autohistory* (Osprey) is very entertaining. The choice is vast and is sure to grow; hopefully these notes will help point the way.

PHOTO GALLERY

1

2

3

1. Flyers of the 'fifties – these are the Jaguar sports cars that the E-type had to live up to: (Right to left) XK120, 1949-54; XK140, 1954-57; and XK150, 1957-60. These examples, owned by Bryan Corser of Shrewsbury, illustrate how the road-going Jaguar sports cars got blander as the decade progressed.

2. When it came to a replacement for the great XK range, Sir William Lyons took a fresh approach. Instead of developing the orthodox XK150, which was rapidly looking old-fashioned as such modern lightweights as the Lotus Elite came along, he looked to his successful Le Mans hat-trick winner for inspiration. (Here Tony Rolt takes the D-type to 2nd place at its Le Mans debut, 1954).

3. The two most important development cars leading up to the E-type were made largely of aluminium: hence their designation E1A and E2A. This is the first, smaller car which was running with a 2.4-litre engine from 1957, photographed by Motor's editor, the late Christopher Jennings, at his West Wales home.

4

5

4. E2A was developed briefly as a competition car, and actually entered by American enthusiast (and Jaguar dealer) Briggs Cunningham for Le Mans in 1960. The car is seen here making its first public appearance earlier that year, at the Le Mans practice session, still unpainted and showing the neat use of rivets ... and the same registration number as E1A!

5. Still untrimmed, the steel prototype poses on the sports field at Jaguar's Browns Lane, Coventry, site. The body shape, originated by Malcolm Sayer for the competition cars, had been adapted very cleverly by Sir

William Lyons to make the 'E' the most spectacular of road cars.

6. Announced in March 1961 as a fixed-head coupe and a roadster, the E-type was unique in its construction. Clearly seen here is the relationship between the front subframe and the bulkhead.

7. First production E-type to be seen in public by the author (then stationed in Ulster) was this Belfast demonstrator being used as course car at the Kirkistown circuit in the spring of 1961. Note the external bonnet

lock. This car has been restored in recent years.

8 & 9. Two views of the beautiful E-type coupe, photographed in contrasting settings. The rear view was taken on the Pic du Midi de Bigorre, high in the Pyrenees, while covering the 1962 Tour de France – an ideal opportunity to discover the joys of E-type motoring. The author reacquainted himself with the same car when he returned to Jaguar the following winter – the hardest for many years. Snow always melted quickly on the E-type's bonnet; triple wipers were standard on the early cars. Note also the grille bar and overriders of the production model.

8

6

7

9

10. Contemporary shot by works photographer Bill Large, taken at Loch an Eilein in the Cairngorms, shows the sleekness and originality of the E-type coupe to good effect.

11. Little external change took place in 1964 when the E-type went from 3.8 to 4.2-litres, except in the boot-badging. This coupe picture was taken at the works.

12. This 4.2 roadster was the best in Britain when Will Athawes (seen with car) was declared national concours champion at the 1978 Town & Country Festival at Stoneleigh.

13

14

13. A good example of a restored 4.2-litre coupe is that of Gordon Skelton (see also colour section). These four Paul Skilleter pictures show the boot and spare wheel well ...

14. ... including the ribs to protect the floor ...

15. ... the original linen-lined toolkit bag and tools ...

16. ... and the triple SU carburetters which made the inlet side of the engine compartment shine so brightly.

17. Later 4.2-litre cars for North America had two Stromberg carburetters as part of the job of meeting the first serious emission-control regulations.

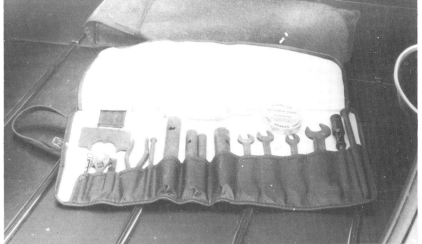

15

16

17

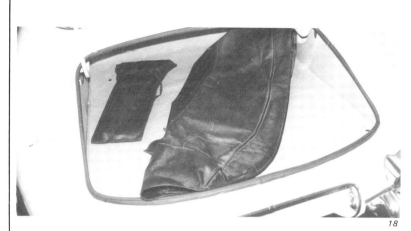

18

18. A disadvantage of the six-cylinder roadsters was the shallow boot, seen here containing wrapped jack and hood cover.

19.   Lockable bootlid-pull and seat-belt mounting in rear bulkhead of late roadster.

20.   Twin fans in 1967-68 export 4.2 E-type.

21. Close-up of rear suspension, showing how driveshaft acts as upper link. This IRS system has been used for all subsequent Jaguars.

22. Unique works composite picture of the 4.2-litre E-type on the production line. The independent rear suspension unit, complete with inboard discs and diff., was built up as a complete assembly, before installation. Likewise, the engine and front suspension were assembled before being offered up to the bulkhead.

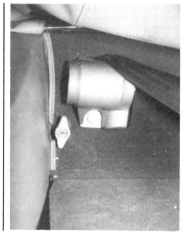

19

20

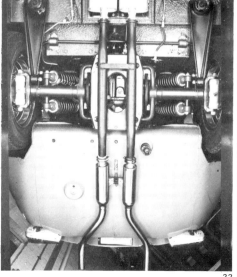

21

22

23

24

25

26

23. The 2+2, introduced in 1966, was a practical solution to the problem of the E-type owner starting a family. An extra nine inches in the wheelbase gave space for two occasional seats, but from some angles the car acquired an ungainly look, and a bright strip was hastily added to the door in an attempt to unscramble the spreading waistline. The roll-top, seen here, was not a factory fitting. This picture was selected for the purpose of comparing the 'saloon' E-type with the roadster and, beyond, a former works long-nose Le Mans D-type – its true ancestor.

24. There was no such thing as a Series "1½", but it is a term which helps describe the gradual changes to the E-type – mainly as new regulations had to be met. The visual 'turning point' came in 1967, when the headlamps had to be moved forward and the covers removed, as on this coupe.

25. Export roadster of the 1967/8 period, with exposed headlamps, and (just visible) the unfortunate number-plate holder required in some markets. (UK owners usually got away with a bonnet-mounted registration number on flexible material).

26. Last-minute surprise of the 1968 London show (following the earlier excitement of the XJ6 announcement) was the Series 2 E-type, which was slipped into Earls Court on the eve of public opening. Note the larger air-intake, the more-protruding headlamps, the new positions for the auxiliary lamps, and (for the first time) the use of pressed-steel wheels – at this stage an optional extra! Less obvious in this view is the improved windscreen rake of the 2+2; this is an export model.

27

28

29

30

31

27. Export model Series 2 coupe, emphasising further protrusion of headlamps.

28. Home-market Series 2 1969/70 roadster still did not have to have side-mounted flashers. Large air-intake still had no grille – just the horizontal bar.

29. Home-market Series 2 2+2 shows heavy-looking new rear lamp mountings.

30. Looking a little further under the Series 2, three of which could be exported in a single container 40 ft. long if the two front cars overlapped like this (Containerisation followed a bad period of transit damage. It was not unusual to hear of a row of cars being pushed along the docks by the one at the end, or of their being parked on ship so close together that the driver walked out across the bonnet or the boot).

31. Late-model Series 2 roadster with left-hand drive for Denis Jenkinson, Motor Sport's Continental Correspondent, seen collecting it (his second E-type after years of Porsche motoring) from Home Sales Distribution Manager David Thorn, right, and the author (then Jaguar's PR man) at the Browns Lane works in 1970. Jenks enjoyed his Jaguars sufficiently to write a book about them!

32

33

34

35

37

38

36

32. 1970 saw Jaguar finalising its Series 3 E-type, which was intended to have the six-cylinder engine and a new V12. It was engineered for both, with a new, broader front subframe to cater for the V12. This picture shows what the XK engine looked like in the new frame; a similar picture was used in the first Series 3 catalogue, but the six-cylinder version was never in fact marketed, although two or three cars run by the works were eventually sold.

33. This picture of a Series 2's engine compartment is used here to compare with the previous one, and shows the relatively tight fit in the frame, whereas a 6-cylinder Series 3 would have had good accessibility.

34. A clever impression of the V12 and Series 3, executed for Jaguar by Autocar artist Gordon Horner.

35. Jaguar's new V12 engine (announced with the Series 3 in March 1971) was not the four-cam which Jaguar's technical chief Bill Heynes preferred, but a 5.3-litre with one camshaft for each bank of cylinders. Gone, too, were the beloved hemispherical combustion chambers, the unit having virtually flat head faces.

36. Impressive new engine in production on purpose-built assembly line at the Radford, Coventry, factory, which Jaguar had acquired (in acquiring Daimler) in 1960 – the home of Britain's only other regular production V12, the 'sleeve-valve' Double Six, some forty years earlier.

37. Installation of V12 engine in Series Three E-type. This engine was the brainchild of Walter Hassan and Harry Mundy.

38. Close-up from roughly the same angle as photo 37, showing ingenious throttle linkage to the four carburetters. (Hassan had hoped the engine would have fuel-injection from the outset, but its arrival was to co-incide with the E-type's obsolescence in 1975.) Note extra ducting on this late car, for injecting air into the combustion area to meet exhaust emission regulations.

39

40

41

42

43

39.   The long wheelbase was standardised for the Series 3, which came as a two-seater roadster or the familiar 2 + 2 (the 2-seat FHC being dropped). Design of the 2 + 2's bootlid ventilator had still not been settled when this picture was taken.

40.   Another view of the Series 3 2 + 2, showing definitive bootlid ventilator and strange effect of widening the wheelarches. The four exhaust pipes played a very gentle tune.

41. Aggressive stance of the Series 3, seen here in roadster form. Note: only two windscreen wipers.

42. The author with a Series 3 roadster, the extra 9 inches making it look very long indeed for a 2-seater. As with Series 2, home-market cars did not have side flashers to start with. Tonneau cover should, by rights, be black. This light-coloured one was being tried-out to reduce the contrast for pastel painted cars.

43. Optional Series 3 hardtop, fitted to export roadster (side flashers and whitewalls).

44. Gone was the woodrim steering wheel, but cockpit still had traditional looks apart from new air-conditioning vents under main instrument panel.

44

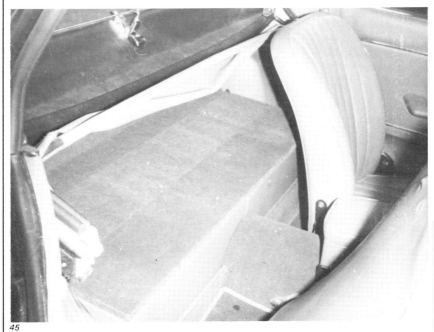

45

46

45. Series 3 roadster had plenty of luggage space behind the seats, unlike the old short-wheelbase models, note flap on shelf floor, beneath which smaller items could be hidden from view.

46. Series Three tool kit: not quite up to the early standards, but still pretty good.

47. Early assignment for the Series 3 (with optional wire wheels and earless hubs) at the 1971 Monaco Grand Prix: Prince Rainier and the late Princess Grace set off to open the course in a works car, watched by, among others, former ace Louis Chiron who raced an XK120 Jaguar at least once, back in the early 'fifties.

48. Same creator, different era – three of Sir William Lyons' great 2-seater sports cars (left to right): XK120, 1949-1954; Swallow-bodied Austin Seven, 1927-1932; and V12 Series 3 E-type, 1971-1975.

47

48

49

50

51

52

53

49. Several pictures were taken with the RAF's co-operation in the early '70s, when the new 'Jaguar' fighter was about to go into service. This shot was never used, and it was said that the engine was damaged in the effort of hoisting the plane over the car; note the retracted undercarriage! No names, no pack drill. After all this time, however, I see no harm in publishing it. The eyes coming out on stalks, watching the mirror fill up, are those of apprentice Tony Bell – one of a number of the old team now happily working at Browns Lane again in its revival years. This particular 2+2 went to BL heritage rather than out to the trade, once its life as a press car was over.

50. £3,000,000 seemed an awful lot of money for Jaguar to spend on its V12 engine manufacturing plant, back in the early '70s. At one time it was thought that the equipment would also be used to make a 60 degree V8 engine, but its inherent imbalance caused that project to be dropped. In 1983, the V12 was still going strong (in XJ12/XJ-S 'HE' form), but the tendency for future Jaguars is towards 6-cylinders, generally.

51. The roadster alone went on into the 1973-75 period, by which time North America required front and rear 'crashability'. The regulation was met by chassis-mounted struts which were hidden behind these ungainly rubber-covered projections.

52. Another view of the last type of 'E' for North America. Even the last few cars managed to avoid these ugly bumpers. Note twin pipes, as opposed to four originally.

53. Though their main panels were made by Abbey Panels of Coventry, the E-type bodies (like those of previous sports models) were built in the Browns Lane bodyshop. It was therefore, quite a moment when the last one was completed in 1974. Left to right are E-type bodyshop foremen Derek Platt, Sidney Salt, and Albert Pickering. Note how headlamp 'tunnels' were carried into the paintshop.

54

54. To make space for saloon production in 1974, (when short-term boss Geoffrey Robinson was announcing plans for a capacity of 80-90,000 Jaguars a year, or more than double any reasonable forecast), E-type production suffered. The last E-types were made on a temporary assembly line in a new storage block at Browns Lane, and with many items in short supply they hung about the factory well into the New Year of 1975. Here is the last E-type, with wire wheels on the front, so that it can be wheeled off the ramp to mark the end of production of one of the greatest sports cars the world has seen.

55. Now with the correct wheels at all four corners, the last E-type poses in the wet with the team that made it. Geoffrey Robinson (Chief Executive, soon to leave for fulltime politics) is towards the centre of the group. Nearest camera are the directors of the Radford and Browns Lane factories respectively, Jack Randle and the late Peter Craig, who did so much to keep Jaguar people's spirits up in the difficult years to follow.

56. Close-up of self-explanatory plate, fitted to dashboard of last E-type, one of fifty finished in black, and retained by the company for posterity, registration number HDU 555N.

57. E-types are not made today, but the front subframe design and running gear have been used to differing degrees to make copies of the legendary D-type, the car from which the E-type was derived ... quite a compliment really. The copy-cars, as built by the unconnected 'Lynx' and 'Deetype' companies, are dealt with in another Super Profile – on the D-type and XKSS. This picture was taken at RS Panels' Nuneaton premises in 1982.

58. Roy Salvadori leads Graham Hill at Oulton Park, April 1961, the E-type's racing debut. Hill was the winner, with Salvadori dropping to third.

55

This is the last car built after thirteen years' manufacture of the Jaguar 'E' Type Sports Cars.

W. Lyons

Chassis No. IS 2872

Sir William Lyons. President. Jaguar Cars. Coventry. 1974.

56   57

58

59   60

59. Graham Hill was the most successful E-type racer of all in the '60s, at international level. Here he is, en route to victory at Silverstone with John Coombs' lightweight car, which was developed in conjunction with the works. Only a very few lightweights were made, and Malcolm Sayer devised a special low-drag top. Only two were made, however, and this picture shows the model in normal '63 racing trim.

60. Throughout the '60s, private owners of standard E-types would adapt them for racing, often dominating their class at club level, as in this typical 'marque' or 'prodsports' event at Brands Hatch, Kent.

61. Twice declared Jaguar Driver of the Year, John Harper was one of the outstanding E-type racers of the early 'seventies when this picture was taken in the Silverstone paddock. His car, like so many others, was prepared by Ron Beaty's Forward Engineering company.

62. 1974 and 1975 saw Lee Mueller and Bob Tullius bring the V12 E-type to life in American sports car racing. Tullius's Group 44 team car was brought back to Britain, and is still demonstrated occasionally. Here it completes several laps of the Donington Park circuit during a Jaguar Drivers' Club race meeting, driven by Jaguar service manager Peter Taylor, himself a highly successful E-type driver in the early 'seventies with his own V12 2+2 coupe.

63. Quite outstanding in recent years has been this much-modified 6-cylinder roadster, described by its owners, Gran Turismo Jaguar, as 'the winningest Jaguar' in the USA. Its English driver Freddy Baker has certainly scored many victories, and in 1980 won an SCCA championship and the Jaguar Driver of the Year award. This picture was taken at the team's local circuit, Nelson Ledges, Ohio, in 1977.

61

62

63

C1

C2

C1. Close-up of the beautiful but vulnerable nose of an early works E-type, with fully enclosed headlamps. Positioning of the front number plate was often a crucial factor in British law.

C2. Roadster close-up showing chromium-plated wire wheels and whitewall tyres preferred for US market. All regular production E-types had wind-up windows.

C3. Early E-type fixed-head coupe: a contemporary shot.

C4. E-type roadster in 'Series 1' form ('Series 1' is a purely retrospective term).

C3

C4

C5

C5. E-type roadster with optional hardtop, seen at the Curborough sprint course in recent times. The wheels are proprietary alloy ones. The driver is Herbert Shepherd, who has been competing and winning with Jaguars for many years.

C6. The so-called 'lightweight' E-type looked much smoother without its bumpers and headlamp surrounds. This former Cunningham team car is seen at Silverstone in recent, restored condition.

C6

C7, 8 & 9. Two exterior views of the superbly restored 1965 4.2-litre 'Series 1' owned by Gordon Skelton. Cockpit shot shows early-type switchery.

C9

C7

C8

C10. Clearly seen are the push-and-twist bonnet-locking handles on each side. (On the first few cars, in 1961, the bonnet locks were external.) Straight-port 'gold' head, triple carburettors, and position of engine in subframe are all clearly visible in this overhead shot of Gordon Skelton's prize-winning car.

C11. Visiting Reims, the scene of so many Jaguar victories, a works 1967 4.2-litre roadster with partially-exposed headlamps.

C12. E-type '2+2' in '67 form (semi-exposed headlamps).

C10

C11

C12

C13. Series 2 4.2-litre '2+2', showing improved rake to windscreen for this 1968 to '70 model.

C14. Interior of early '2+2' (1966-7), showing toggle switches preferred by some drivers. This is the optional automatic transmission model.

C15. 1967/8 export specification roadster featuring tumbler switches, recessed heater controls, and other concessions to 'safety'.

C16. Remarkably little change in the cockpit of a 1974/5 Series 3 roadster, apart from the smaller steering wheel. (This is the very last E-type to have been built, and has been retained by Jaguar.)

C13

C14

C15

C16

C17

C17. Well-filled bonnet of the Series 3 (V12) E-type; this is the very last E-type, which was retained by Jaguar.

C18. Almost a change of character: The Series 3 E-type looked more aggressive than its predecessors, with its grille and extra air intake.

C18

C19

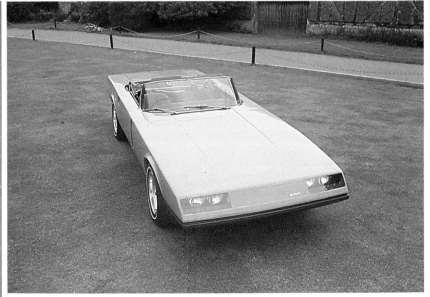

C20

C19. Most successful six-cylinder E-type in the USA, this car entered by Gran Turismo Jaguar of Eastlake, Ohio, prepared by Lou Fidanza, and driven by Freddy Baker, has won innumerable races, culminating in the 1980 SCCA Championships at Road Atlanta.

C20. Special bodies are rare on E-types. One, by Bertone, was a Daily Telegraph "ideal car" project for the 1967 London show. It was auctioned by Sotheby-Parke-Bernet at Boston, Massachusetts, the following Spring. The Guyson-E V12, pictured here, was created by William Towns, the freelance designer, in the early 1970s; the integrated look of the original has been lost in retention of the standard screen; slab-sided body was in fact fitted over original panelling!